She replaced the receiver with the uneasy feeling that the phone call had been a big mistake. Something was definitely odd here. Yet he had seemed so pleasant at first—

Until he found out who she was.

Now what did *that* say?

She briefly comforted herself with the thought that perhaps he wouldn't come after all. He'd sounded more astonished and resentful than concerned about her predicament. But in less than five minutes a vehicle roared into the driveway. A moment later the front door opened.

"Kat?" The sound of the tense male voice erased a tiny hope that the vehicle might be Mrs. L. returning early.

Her fingers dug into the carpet as her apprehension climbed like a panicked cat scrambling up a tree. This was no eerie, imagined moment of irrational fear. This was real. She was trapped, vulnerable, flat-on-her-back helpless. And she'd blithely informed a total stranger of this. She jammed a knuckle against her mouth. She wouldn't respond to his call. Maybe he'd go away—

No, not going away.

Footsteps crossed the polished hardwood floor of the living room. A spot in the floor beside the staircase creaked. And then a tanned hand and muscular arm shoved the bedroom door open wide.

Forgotten

A PALISADES CONTEMPORARY ROMANCE

Forgotten

LORENA McCOURTNEY

PALISADES

This is a work of fiction. The characters, incidents, and dialogues are products of
the author's imagination and are not to be construed as real. Any resemblance to
actual events or persons, living or dead, is entirely coincidental.

FORGOTTEN
published by Palisades
a division of Multnomah Publishers, Inc.

© 1998 by Lorena McCourtney
International Standard Book Number: 1-57673-222-3

Cover illustration by C. Michael Dudash
Design by Brenda McGee

Scripture quotations are from:
The Holy Bible, New International Version (NIV)
© 1973, 1984 by International Bible Society,
used by permission of Zondervan Publishing House

Printed in the United States of America

For information:
MULTNOMAH PUBLISHERS, INC.
POST OFFICE BOX 1720
SISTERS, OREGON 97759

Library of Congress Cataloging-in-Publication Data:
McCourtney, Lorena.
Forgotten/by Lorena McCourtney.   p. cm.
ISBN 1–57673–222–3 (paper)
I. Title.
PS3563.C3449F67 1998   97–32393
813'.54—dc21   CIP

98 99 00 01 02 03 04 — 10 9 8 7 6 5 4 3 2 1

Are not five sparrows sold for two pennies?
Yet not one of them is forgotten by God.

LUKE 12:6

One

She slashed words across the paper quickly, writing so fast that her injured hand cramped. This time, she hoped, momentum would keep the stream of information flowing.

Rain is falling outside my window. I hear waves crashing on the beach. I had meat loaf and strawberry Jell-O for lunch. And tea, unsweetened. I don't like sweet tea. I'm in the Benton Beach Community Hospital. A telephone is ringing down the hall. My doctor's name is Fischer, Emily Fischer, and my name is—

Her hand halted in midsentence, stopped by the power outage in the brain behind it, helpless as a rocket with a missing guidance system. Her little game to trick her subconscious into revealing its secrets had failed again. In savage frustration she crumpled the useless paper and hurled it across the room.

Dr. Fischer ducked the flying missile as she stepped through the door. "That was a rather powerful throw," she observed, not unkindly, as she retrieved the crumpled ball. "Perhaps in your other life you were a pitcher for the Yankees."

"Or maybe I was a pauper or a princess or a preacher. Who knows?" The useless anger collapsed, but despair seeped into her voice even as she managed a smile and massaged her cramped hand. Silently she added, no, not a princess. If she were a princess, surely someone would be looking for her. And, apparently, no one was.

The absence of a past created a lonely present.

Both the local police chief and a friendly, gray-haired woman from the *Benton Beach Weekly* had come to look her over and record her vital statistics. Age, between twenty-one and twenty-six; height, five feet ten inches; weight (after a guesstimate to subtract the weight of the cast), one-hundred-thirty pounds; hair, blond; eyes, blue; skin, fair; no identifying scars or tattoos. The police chief had later reported that she didn't match the description of anyone on his missing-person or wanted-criminal reports.

"It will all come back to you eventually." Dr. Fischer, smelling faintly of antiseptic and a fresh, apple-blossom cologne, squeezed her wrist reassuringly while automatically checking her pulse. "Be patient."

"But when? *When?* It's been over a week now, and it's like standing on the edge of a bottomless pit when I try to look farther back than that." She hesitated. "Except…"

Dr. Fischer's kind, blue-gray gaze sharpened. "Except what?"

"Except that I keep having this nagging feeling that I've forgotten something really important, something I *must* remember, something I have to do—" She broke off as she realized the absurdity of that statement. Yes, she'd forgotten something. She'd forgotten her entire *life*.

Dr. Fischer didn't pass off the nagging feeling as ridiculous, however. "I'm no psychologist, but that could be significant," she said thoughtfully. She leaned forward, a lock of silvering blond hair falling across her cheek. "It could indicate an emotional component to your memory loss, perhaps something your mind doesn't want to accept or acknowledge, and these injuries became a convenient excuse to tuck it away."

"Which means I may be a mental case as well as a physical wreck."

"No, you are not a mental case! You're bright, intelligent, and personable. You have no hallucinations, no paranoia, no irrational or inappropriate behavior—" Dr. Fischer's tone was almost fierce until, in the easy camaraderie that had grown up between them, she added teasingly, "Until you start throwing things, of course."

She smiled guilty acknowledgment. "What does everyone call me, since I don't have a name?"

"Nothing very original, I'm afraid. Usually 'the Jane Doe in 111.' Is there something you'd *like* to be called?"

The young woman on the hospital bed closed her eyes and mentally tiptoed backward. She wobbled on the edge of the dark hole within her mind, desperately reaching for *something*, then opened her eyes in defeat. Her gaze flicked to the window. "Robin. I'd like to be called...Robin."

Dr. Fischer's gaze followed the young woman's to the red-breasted bird perched on the branch of a gnarled pine outside the window. "Robin it is then," she agreed briskly. "So, Robin, how's the headache today?"

"Much better." The newly named Robin cautiously fingered the crescent of stitches curving from her left temple to the back of her head, winced, and explored another zigzag of sutures on the opposite side. "Now my scalp just feels tight and itchy."

"That's normal."

"But *I'm* not normal! I didn't know what day or year it was when I woke up here, and I got the president wrong; but I knew from the very first minute, from the very *scent*, that I was in a hospital. *How?* I can read and write. I know about tea and telephones, all the everyday clutter of life. But I don't know anything about *me.*"

"Memory is a complicated thing," Dr. Fischer said noncommittally. She smoothed the crumpled paper. "You know you don't like sweet tea."

"Not until I tasted it yesterday. When I also discovered I'm not fond of the broccoli they seem to have in oversupply here." She wrinkled her nose, then leaned back against the raised hospital bed and smiled guiltily. "I'm sorry. I sound like a

11

spoiled brat, don't I? It's just so frustrating and frightening." She pleated the sheet over the lumpy outline of the cast that immobilized her left leg from foot to thigh. "I've forgotten everything important. And I also *feel* forgotten."

The doctor's warm hug was motherly. "I know."

For a moment, Robin clung to her, feeling like a lost child, helpless and vulnerable. She battled a gathering of tears before forcing herself to pull away and ask, "Do my tests show anything?" Over the last few days she had been examined, x-rayed, scanned, and imaged with every diagnostic tool the limited facilities of this small hospital on the southern Oregon coast had to offer.

Dr. Fisher flipped through the papers on her clipboard. "We don't have the equipment for some of the more sophisticated tests, but we've covered the basics. Your concussion was severe, and your scalp has enough stitches to make a quilting bee proud, but there's no blood in your cerebrospinal fluid, and your slight cerebral edema—that's brain swelling—is gone. The leg is broken, of course, but the bone didn't puncture the skin, which is a blessing, as is the fact that little water got in your lungs. The good Lord must have been looking out for you."

No, if the Lord were good and looking out for her, she wouldn't be here injured and forgotten, Robin thought with resentment.

"I know the injury to the tendon on your right hand makes using the hand awkward, but it will heal. As will your numerous bruises, cuts, and black eye—" Dr. Fischer flipped the clipboard to align the pages and glanced up. "Which at this point is an interesting abstract of pea green and sulfur yellow. What I'm saying is that basically you're young and healthy and will heal quickly."

"Healing is more than mending physically."

"A philosopher as well as a potential pitcher." Dr. Fischer

smiled and exaggerated a wise nod. "But perhaps, when the psychologist in the county mental health department returns from vacation, she can offer some insight into your problems."

Robin absentmindedly fingered the line of stitches on her head again, the short buzz cut a velvet bristle against her palm.

Dr. Fischer noticed the gesture and smiled. "Sorry about the haircut. I wasn't concerned about giving you anything stylish before I sewed you up. Your hair was so long and tangled and matted with blood and seawater that I had to get rid of it in a hurry."

"It doesn't matter. I don't have any debutante balls or elegant cocktail parties planned."

A secretary from the front office stepped through the door and handed the doctor a slip of paper. She read the message and then looked up at Robin. "But you do have a visitor coming tomorrow."

Robin leaned forward. "A *visitor?* Someone who knows me?"

"Maybe. Police Chief Derrickson got a call from a man down in San Francisco. Someone sent him a copy of our local newspaper with the photo and article about you in it. He thinks you may be his missing wife."

Wife? Robin sank back against the raised hospital bed, shocked. She lifted her left hand and spread her fingers wonderingly. Did the rough scratches conceal the pale line where a wedding band had once been? The possibility wasn't illogical, of course.

Yet somehow it had simply never occurred to her that she might be someone's *wife.*

Two

He was in the hallway. She could hear the two sets of footsteps approaching, the lower, male voice alternating with Dr. Fischer's higher-pitched, more rapid words. The doctor sounded nervous, Robin thought. But not half as nervous as *she* was. She rubbed her damp palms against the sheet. Was she about to meet her *husband?*

He paused in the doorway, a head taller than petite Dr. Fischer. Dark hair glittering with raindrops, unsmiling mouth, clenched fists, intense eyes that bored into Robin's like dark lasers. Had she done something terrible to him, she wondered in sudden dismay. Something beyond simply disappearing?

"This is our patient, known as Robin. Robin…Stanton Riker." Dr. Fischer hovered protectively by the hospital bed, one hand on Robin's shoulder.

Stanton Riker was, in an austere way, good-looking, midthirties, dressed in an impeccable dark suit that murmured money and conservative taste. He did not rush to embrace Robin in instant recognition. She self-consciously tugged at a wisp of hair behind her ear as his gaze probed her. She couldn't remember having long hair, but now she was uncomfortably aware of having almost *no* hair. Was this a man she loved, she wondered uneasily. A man to whom she had promised her life?

"She was found on the beach nearby?" His gaze remained on Robin, but he turned his head to direct the question to Dr. Fischer. It appeared he assumed Robin's loss of memory meant other mental deficiencies as well.

The doctor hesitated before answering, as if she found this

assumption arrogant and insensitive. "Yes, nine days ago, on a secluded beach where transients often camp out. Two of them found her, badly injured and unconscious. Since regaining consciousness here in the hospital a day later, she has no memory of who she is or how she came to be on the beach. She had no identification, and no car was found on the highway nearby."

Robin knew Dr. Fischer didn't intend it that way, but the story came out sounding faintly unsavory. Transients. No identification. No car. Not a muscle moved in Stanton Riker's coldly handsome face, yet Robin sensed his distaste.

"Drugs?" he asked.

"No trace of drugs or alcohol," Dr. Fischer said emphatically.

"Can she speak, so I can hear her voice?"

"Of course I can speak!" Robin snapped. "I've lost my memory, not my intelligence or vocal cords."

His eyes flared briefly, as if a dumb animal had just spoken to him. He offered no apology, but he did then address Robin directly. "Am I at all familiar to you?"

"No. Am I at all familiar to *you?*"

His answer was black-ice smooth, emotionless. "Your facial structure is similar to my wife's, but the bruises and clipped hair make identification problematic. Your voice doesn't sound like Tricia's, but I haven't spoken to her in over a year. I'm a corporate attorney with a large chemical firm, and she disappeared while I was away on business. The disappearance has created awkward complications."

Robin and Dr. Fischer exchanged surreptitious glances. The "complications" sounded more important to Stanton Riker than the missing wife herself. Robin jerked when he reached for her hand, then reluctantly let him lift and inspect it. His hand was cool, smooth, and dry. Hers trembled, like a moth in a spiderweb.

"You have Tricia's hands," he said thoughtfully. "Long, slender fingers, elegantly shaped nails."

The hands were less than elegant now, scratched and battered, nails clipped with more efficiency than style. She snatched her hand back and clenched both hands into fists, burying the nails against her palms. She didn't want to be—

"But you aren't Tricia." He spoke decisively, no reasons cited, case simply closed. Robin's hands opened limply with relief. He turned to Dr. Fischer, thanked her for her time and assistance, and departed without looking back.

Dr. Fischer dashed to the door and closed it behind him. She leaned against it, clipboard clutched to her chest. "Praise the Lord!"

She rushed back to the bed and hugged Robin, and then they were half giggling, half crying, like two children in mischievous conspiracy. In spite of an undercurrent of disappointment that she still didn't know who she was, the fact that she wasn't Tricia Riker flooded Robin with giddy relief. Finally the doctor straightened and shook her head.

"Slide a stick down that man's back and you'd have an Armani-suited Popsicle," she declared.

Robin giggled, but she shivered in spite of the laughter. "Would I have *had* to go with him if he'd identified me as his wife?"

Dr. Fischer blinked as if startled by the question. "No, of course not." Then she hesitated, as if she wasn't positive of her quick answer after all, as if there could be unknown legal complications.

"I can't just stay here at the hospital indefinitely. I must be running up an enormous bill."

"You can come home with me for a while," said Dr. Fischer.

Robin was stunned. "Oh, but I couldn't!"

"You most certainly could," the doctor insisted. "I'll put you to work organizing the files in my medical library. Oh, but under the dazzle of Stanton Riker's charismatic presence—" Dr. Fischer rolled her eyes at that facetious description of the iceman. "I almost forgot to tell you some big news! Mrs. Sanders at the newspaper says that Associated Press has picked up your story, and your photo is going to be in newspapers all across the country! Someone will surely see and recognize you soon."

Robin uneasily stretched the sheet over her cast. That was good news, of course, yet... "But what if some man comes along and says I'm his wife. How do we know if he's telling the truth?"

"I can't imagine why anyone would—" Dr. Fischer stopped short. "Well, that's naïve, isn't it? The world is full of people with thoughts more evil and devious than you and I can possibly imagine, I'm afraid."

Robin swallowed. "I feel like a lost puppy, waiting for my owner to come and claim me."

Yet even as she said that she collided with another thought that occasionally skittered through her mind. Was it possible there was a life behind her to which something inside her did not *want* to return, some situation that she had frantically tried to escape? Had she perhaps done something so appalling that her mind refused to acknowledge it? Yet there was also that recurring, nagging feeling that she'd forgotten something of vital importance that she *must* remember.

So confusing. All so desperately confusing.

"We will make certain only the proper 'owner' claims you," Dr. Fischer declared firmly. "He'll have to have definite proof to show."

~ ~ ~ ~ ~

Such cautious steps did not appear necessary, however. No line formed to claim the woman in room 111. The photo and article appeared in a number of newspapers nationwide, but the coverage was not as extensive as it might have been had an earthquake not rumbled across southern California, creating an outpouring of human-interest stories to capture the media's attention. Police Chief Derrickson's office received a dozen or so inquiries about Robin, but only two middle-aged couples showed up to look at her. The first rejected her in less than two minutes, angry that the photo had been "deceptive." The second couple was more tactful, but she was a disappointment to them also.

"One lost puppy, still unclaimed," Robin said after they were gone. She tried to keep her voice light, even amused, but she knew the attempt was hollow. She shifted in the upholstered chair near the window, rigid leg propped on a footstool. This was where she spent much of her time now, when she wasn't practicing with crutches. The window was open on this sunny and breezy spring day, a tang of sea air mingling with the heavier hospital scents of antiseptic and soap and today's stew.

Dr. Fischer patted Robin's arm sympathetically and a little helplessly. "I'm sorry. Look, I know you rejected this suggestion earlier, but letting Pastor Ross come by really might be helpful. He's a wonderful man, so easy to talk to—"

"No!" Robin didn't have to seek the answer. It sprang up like an armed guard, powerful and unyielding. *No entrance here!* Then, feeling guilty after all the doctor's help and personal attention she'd accepted, she softened the rejection fractionally. "Maybe later."

"Okay. Anytime."

"Isn't there something we could do to jolt my memory? Give it a jump start or something?"

"I've been trying to give myself a crash course in amnesia," Dr. Fischer admitted. "But it's a tenuous area. Hypnosis has been used, and there are drugs that induce an altered mental state in which repressed memories may surface."

Mind-altering drugs. Hypnosis. Robin shivered in instant aversion.

"But neither drug intervention nor hypnosis has been particularly successful with amnesia, and I really think *time* is our most effective tool. From what I understand, lost memory may dribble back in bits and pieces, or there may be one sudden, dramatic breakthrough." The doctor hesitated before adding reluctantly, "Although there have been a few rare cases in which lost memory never returned."

Two more days. Robin couldn't see that her hair was making any faster comeback than her memory, although Dr. Fischer assured her it was. The stitches in her scalp had been removed with the warning that she wasn't to do any tugging or pulling in that delicate area. Later today she would be moving to the doctor's home, and the generous doctor had already supplied new clothes to replace the shredded ones in which she'd been found.

This morning Robin was working out with the crutches again, following a horseshoe pattern back and forth around her bed and practicing turns. She'd spent a restless night. For some reason the possibility that the black hole in her mind held some appalling secret about her past had preyed on her all night, even outweighing the fear that her memory might never return.

She was just negotiating the tricky maneuver of the turn when a voice at the door said uncertainly, "Kathryn?"

Robin lifted her gaze from keeping track of feet, cast, and crutches. The woman who peered cautiously through the doorway was sixtyish, gray-haired, her face wrinkled but rosy, figure sturdy in pink polyester pants. Slowly, almost hesitantly she moved closer, until she was peering directly up into Robin's face, her blue eyes behind bifocals searching. Almost wonderingly she reached up and fingertipped Robin's cropped hair.

"Oh, Kathryn, your hair…your beautiful hair! But it is you, isn't it?" Then she smiled, a smile that lit up her worn face with radiance. "Yes, it is. Kat, it really is you!"

The crutches trembled in Robin's hands. "*You know me?*"

"I wasn't positive when I saw the picture in the Sacramento newspaper, but now that I'm here—Of course I know you. Oh, Kat, sweetie, it's so good to see you! I know you said you wanted to get away and think for a while, but I was getting worried when I didn't hear from you for so long." Her bifocaled gaze took in the cast and stitches, and her tone gently scolded when she added, "Apparently with good reason."

"Are you…my mother?"

"Oh, no, honey, I'm not your sweet mother—" The woman shook her head regretfully, gray hair wisping around her ears. "You really don't remember, do you?"

"No."

"Maybe we should sit down."

The woman, who acted as if she'd had experience at this sort of thing, gently helped Robin…*Kat?*…to the upholstered chair, eased the immobilized leg onto the footstool, and briskly located a folding metal chair in the corner for herself. She pulled it up close, bringing a clean-scrubbed scent of soap mingled with a hint of vanilla.

"I hardly know where to start. I'm Lenore Lennox?" She

21

offered the name on a questioning note, as if hoping it meant something to the young woman in the chair. When Robin shook her head regretfully, she went on. "I've been your parents' cook and housekeeper for years. I don't know how else to break this to you—They're dead, Kat. Thornton and Mavis, they died last summer, August second."

Her parents were dead. Even though she couldn't remember them, a pang of loss opened a great, fresh emptiness inside. Was this the emotional shock she'd desperately tried to block with her loss of memory? Yet at the moment another question overrode even this harsh news. She leaned forward, hands clamped tensely around the arms of the chair. "Mrs. Lennox, there's something I have to know—"

"Mrs. L. That's what you've always called me. Mrs. L."

"Mrs. L., before I disappeared, did I do something terrible, something unforgivable?"

Mrs. L.'s bright blue eyes widened, startled. "*You?* Oh, no, sweetie, of course not! You were just so confused and uncertain about your career and life, and terribly broken up about your parents' deaths." She patted Robin's knee comfortingly.

Relief about this single element of her past—she hadn't done anything horrible after all!—was so huge, so overwhelming, that if the weighty cast hadn't held her down, she'd have stood up and danced. She sobered instantly, however, remembering the sad fact about her parents. "How did they die?"

"Their small plane crashed on take-off right there at the ranch, and they were killed instantly. Their bodies were cremated and the ashes shipped back to Virginia where your mother had family buried."

She squeezed her eyes shut, desperately willing herself to remember. She felt an emptiness of loss, yes, a desperate emptiness, but no sense of personal involvement with these people so tragically killed.

Hesitantly she murmured aloud the names the woman had called her, tentatively trying them on for size. "Kathryn. Kat." The first felt too formal. The second jarred, like a squawk over a loudspeaker. She'd grown comfortable with *Robin* and felt an unexpected reluctance to let it go. "What's my last name?"

"Why, Cavanaugh, of course."

Then another thought struck her, an apprehension that had lingered ever since her almost marriage to the icy Stanton Riker. "Am I married?"

"No. Although I think you've been engaged half a dozen times." Mrs. L. laughed indulgently, although that past sounded rather flighty and frivolous to Robin. Mrs. L. started rummaging in a floppy straw bag she carried in addition to a pink purse. "I grabbed a few pictures out of the old photo albums and brought them along. You can go through everything when you get home, of course, but I thought perhaps these would bring something back to you."

Photos! Oh, yes. She reached for them eagerly. "Do I have brothers and sisters?"

Mrs. L. shook her head. "No, there's just you. Your folks were in their forties before you were born. They said they got the grand prize then, why try again? Actually, I think they were rather in awe of what they'd produced in you, so tall and beautiful and elegant."

She knew she was tall, of course, but it hadn't occurred to her to think of the almost bald scalp and swollen, bruised face that looked back at her from the mirror as *beautiful*.

She studied the photos wonderingly. They showed a pretty blond girl twirling as a ringleted little ballerina, blowing candles at a birthday party, smiling beside a handsome boy at a high school prom, serious in a formal portrait. One showed her in graduation cap and gown standing between two smiling, shorter people, their arms linked around her waist.

"That's you with Thornton and Mavis, of course. Your father was an inventor. He always passed it off as just 'puttering,' but various companies paid him lots of money for all the wonderful little gadgets he thought up. Your mother was creative, too. She wrote fascinating children's books. I first went to work for them back east, when you were just a little tyke. Later I left to go into hospital work, but when they decided to move out to the ranch in northern California, I accepted their offer to work for them again." Mrs. L. dug in the floppy bag again. "Here's something else."

A strange wave of awe rolled through her as she looked at the document. It was an original birth certificate from an eastern state. *Kathryn Anne Cavanaugh*. The date made her twenty-four now, but it was the lock of soft baby hair that really made her breath catch. *Her* hair! Even more than the photos, it made her feel *rooted*, a person with a name and past, not just an unknown who'd borrowed her name from a bird in a tree.

Mrs. L. handed her more pictures, but these weren't glossy photos. These were slick pages cut from magazines.

"What are these?" Kat asked, puzzled. One was a shampoo ad, the model's long hair flowing down her bare back like a sleek golden waterfall, her face coquettishly half turned to the camera. Another page with torn edges showed a sophisticated woman in a high fashion layout, face pouty as she dragged an expensive coat. Yet another magazine page advertising a perfume showed the same woman behind a leather-jacketed man on a motorcycle, smile flashing, long legs provocatively exposed beneath skimpy leather shorts.

Mrs. L. beamed. "Don't you recognize yourself, sweetie? That's you! After, as you always grumbled, hairdressers and makeup and clothes people spent half a day making you look like someone else."

Dr. Fischer rushed in, white coat slightly askew. "I just

heard someone was here—" She'd been doubly protective ever since the encounter with Stanton Riker, and she eyed Mrs. L. suspiciously.

"Look." Kat thrust everything at her, photos, birth certificate, magazine pages. "My name is Kathryn Cavanaugh. Except I go by 'Kat.'"

Dr. Fischer studied everything, her frowning gaze jumping back and forth between photos and her patient while Kat explained about her parents and who Mrs. L. was. Then, almost as if she were a lawyer grilling a hostile witness, the doctor snapped questions at the housekeeper. How long had Kathryn Cavanaugh been missing? Had Mrs. Lennox reported her disappearance? Where was this ranch?

Kat had been gone about three months, Mrs. L. said. After her parents' deaths she'd returned to her career in New York, but several months later she'd come back to the ranch. She'd stayed a couple of weeks, then asked Mrs. L. to take her into Redding to meet some friends.

"I didn't report her missing because she wasn't, really. She was gone, of course, but she'd said she wanted to get away and think for a while. She didn't say how long she'd be away. I was just supposed to look after the place until she returned."

"Did you see these 'friends'?" Dr. Fischer's tone put the word in suspicious quotation marks. "Were they male or female?"

"I didn't see anyone. She had me leave her at a restaurant. They were supposed to meet her there."

"That explains why I didn't have a car when I was found," Kat pointed out. "I was with these friends." Not the most admirable of friends, however, if they'd abandoned her on an isolated beach without identification. Although that was perhaps accusing them unjustly. Purse or billfold could simply have been lost while she was sloshing in the surf.

"This ranch you want to take Robin—my patient to. There

are what, cowboys there? A manager?"

"Oh, no. Just me. A handyman from across the road helps me out occasionally. And there are my cats, of course, Maggie and Tillie. Actually, it isn't really a *ranch*, although we always call it that. It's just a lovely eighty acres of trees and meadow and river hidden back in the mountains. Thornton and Mavis liked it out there by themselves in the middle of nature." Mrs. L.'s sturdy fingers twisted the knee of her pink pants and occasionally pushed nervously at her glasses.

"I'm doubtful about my patient being so far away from proper medical care." Dr. Fischer frowned, then looked at Kat. "And I really think you should see the psychologist—"

"You said yourself that time was the best healer." Kat felt a little sorry for the housekeeper. Who wouldn't feel uncomfortable under Dr. Fischer's machine-gun onslaught of suspicious questions! "And Mrs. L. has worked in a hospital with patients herself."

"Really." Dr. Fischer didn't sound convinced.

"Have you any idea how long before Kat regains her memory?" Mrs. L. asked.

"It could be a few days or weeks or months. It could be never," the doctor added with what Kat felt was almost too-brutal honesty.

Mrs. L. did not seem dismayed, however. "That doesn't matter," she said firmly. "We'll manage."

Kat quirked a finger to bring Dr. Fischer closer so she could whisper in her ear. "I don't think she's planning to carry me off to some evil den of iniquity."

Dr. Fischer glanced over her shoulder at Mrs. L., who was perched on her metal chair looking rather like an anxious, pink-polyester-clad bird. Finally the doctor grinned a little sheepishly. "I'm acting like an overprotective hen with a lone chick, aren't I?"

"I appreciate your concern."

Dr. Fischer picked up the magazine pages again. "I should have guessed. So tall and slim and long-legged, so beautiful and elegant. And those spectacular cheekbones! What else could you be but a model? Would you believe, that's the very same shampoo I use?" She smiled with the old tease. "May I have your autograph, O famous one?"

The reality was just beginning to sink in with Kat. She was a *model*, apparently a fairly successful one. She didn't *feel* like a model. Which didn't mean anything, of course, she thought ruefully. She didn't feel like anything else, either.

"I'd really like to start home as soon as possible." Mrs. L. sounded both anxious and apologetic. "I don't like to be on the road after dark."

"What about my hospital bill?" Kat asked Dr. Fischer. "And your bill, too, of course."

"I'll chalk mine up to research. You're the most interesting case I've had in years," Dr. Fischer said generously. "And sometimes the hospital simply has to write off certain debts as uncollectable—"

"Oh, we can pay! The household money ran out," Mrs. L. sounded apologetic about that, too, "but I have a little money of my own that Thornton and Mavis left me. I could—" she dug a checkbook out of the pink purse—"give the hospital fifteen hundred dollars. Would that be enough to start with? Then Kat can send the rest when we get home."

Kat blinked. "I can?"

"Why, yes, I'm sure you can. Your folks weren't jet-set rich, but they were well off, and you inherited everything except the money I received. There's a stack of envelopes from banks and a stockbroker waiting for you at home. And you own the ranch, too, of course."

Kat looked at Dr. Fischer. The doctor was studying Mrs. L.

with a slight frown, as if she were still vaguely suspicious. Then, apparently giving herself a mental shake, she turned back to Kat and smiled. "It looks as if I won't have free labor to put my medical library in order after all."

"There's just one thing—" Both Mrs. L. and Dr. Fischer looked at Kat as if expecting some portentous announcement of suddenly reclaimed memory. "Would you mind calling me Katy? I just don't feel comfortable with Kat."

Mrs. L. beamed again, the look that turned her plain face radiant. "That would be wonderful! We called you Katy when you were a little tyke, but when you got older you wanted to be Kat because it was more 'sophisticated.' But I'm glad you're going back to Katy."

Mrs. L. went down the hall to see about the bill. For the first time in her short memory, Katy, with Dr. Fischer's help, put on nonhospital clothes, including a jaunty blue hat the doctor had provided to cover up her buzzed-off hair. With a certain amazement, she thought about the fact that when she arrived in the hospital she had no name at all, and now she was overflowing with them. Robin. Kathryn. Kat. And now the one that really felt…well, not *familiar*, but snug, like a good fit. Katy. Katy Cavanaugh.

And Katy Cavanaugh, one lost puppy now claimed, was going home.

Three

They drove out of Benton Beach in Mrs. L.'s six-year-old Honda, both loaded with instructions from Dr. Fischer, Katy clutching an additional sheaf of pages detailing her bill. The doctor had taken the phone number at the ranch and said she'd call with the name of a doctor for Katy to see in California.

They crossed the wildly beautiful coast mountains to hit the main north-south interstate over the Siskiyou Mountains into California, where massive Mt. Shasta floated like a snow-clad fantasy above a fluffy skirt of clouds. Mrs. L. chattered cheerfully, bringing to life the past of a close-knit family that sounded wonderful to Katy. Pets, vacations both happy and comically disastrous, holidays with big turkey dinners and Christmas trees and mounds of presents. How could all this be missing from her mind? she wondered, angry and frustrated with herself.

"What about you, Mrs. L.? Don't you have family of your own?"

"Oh, my, yes. I was married once. That's why I'm *Mrs.* L., of course. About all I remember of that annoying man is that he—ugh—ate ketchup on everything, including fried eggs." Mrs. L. wrinkled her nose, then laughed. "But he did give me my wonderful son, my Evan. Evan is an executive with a big company down in Dallas, Texas, that has a nationwide line of franchised dry-cleaning establishments. I don't get to see him as much as I'd like, but he visits me whenever he's up this way on business. I just wish he'd stop working so hard and take time to pick a wife so I could be a grandma one of these days."

She smiled fondly even as she fretted about her son's workaholic tendencies.

"Do I know him?"

"Oh my, yes. He's a couple of years older, but as little tykes, you two were inseparable." She laughed. "When you weren't clobbering each other, of course. Typical kids."

"I'm sorry I can't remember him." Or anything else. Momentarily dispirited, Katy stared off into the distance, where the spire of a church rose above a tiny town tucked into the folded hills. "Did we go to church as a family?"

"Well, Easter and Christmas, although your folks weren't really regular churchgoers. But they were always very generous in helping people and donating to worthwhile charities."

"So they didn't have some big opposition to religion?" Katy remembered her own instant hostility toward Dr. Fischer's Pastor Ross.

"Oh, no, nothing like that."

They turned off the interstate, passing through a few tiny, grocery-gas-and-post-office towns, but the country grew ever more wild and rugged as the paved road narrowed and then turned to gravel. Log trucks occasionally roared by, trailing clouds of dust and the heady tang of freshly cut timber. Creeks danced down mountainsides and plunged over boulders in the brushy ravines; prolific blackberry bushes crowded the road, and oak and sleek-barked shrubs that Mrs. L. called manzanita vied with fir and pine for space and sunlight on the hillsides. Occasionally they passed modest farmhouses set in the midst of a few cleared acres, but after turning off the main gravel road, even those signs of civilization vanished.

Once, crossing a wooden bridge, a sharp apprehension jarred Katy as she looked down at whitewater thundering over huge boulders below, but she recognized the logical source even though it was something else she couldn't remember. She'd been found in the surf-lashed rocks on the coast; her subconscious undoubtedly recognized dangerous, rough-water similarities here even if her conscious mind couldn't remember.

The setting of the house was exactly as Mrs. L. had described, lush green meadow surrounded by thick forest, with masses of juniper and other shrubs framing the log house. But this was no primitive log cabin. This log house was two stories, central front portion all glass soaring from floor to ceiling, heavy wooden railings bordering wide decks. The steeply sloped metal roof was the same rich color as the russet bark of the manzanita, with elegant skylights gilded by the setting sun to islands of gold.

Neither was the house as lonely and isolated as Katy had begun to expect after their long drive through the wilds. Across the road a carved wooden sign swung between two tall, weathered poles: Damascus Boys Ranch. Beyond the rail fence, lawns, garden, and orchard surrounded a neat compound of dark brown buildings. A sweet scent of wood smoke hung in the air, a lazy haze of it drifting on the meadow, and the shouts of unseen boys suggested that somewhere beyond the buildings a lively ball game was in progress.

"What's that?" Katy asked.

"It's a Christian ranch school for problem boys. When we first came I was afraid the boys might be troublemakers, sneaking across the road to do who-knows-what, but there's never been a problem. Then I worried maybe it was run by some weird cult, but they seem normal enough." Mrs. L. shook her head and laughed. "Dyed-in-the-wool worrier, that's me."

"I'm glad you worried that the battered woman in a newspaper photo might be me, or I'd still be on the Oregon coast wondering who I am."

31

Mrs. L. reached across the seat and squeezed Katy's hand. "You're my family, too, you know, every bit as much as my Evan."

With her crutches, Katy maneuvered up the three steps to the front deck, Mrs. L. solicitously hovering over her every awkward clump of the way. Once inside, she leaned heavily on the crutches, only then realizing how exhausted she was after the long day in which her life had changed so drastically.

"You sit down and rest." Mrs. L. patted her arm with motherly concern. "I'll turn the heat on. These spring days are warm, but it's still chilly at night here, and we don't want you catching cold. Then I'll fix a bite to eat."

Katy dropped her crutches on the colorful Navajo rug and gratefully eased into a soft chair. The interior of the house was as impressive as the outside, and Mrs. L. had done a fine, conscientious job of taking care of everything during Katy's absence. Lush ferns and ivy trailed from planters hung around the windows. A huge, river-rock fireplace dominated one corner, its mantel a single thick slab of polished redwood, with a massive chimney rising to the vaulted ceiling above. The hardwood floor, beyond the central square of Navajo rug, gleamed with polish, and red and turquoise pillows scattered on the ivory leather furniture picked up the colors of the rug. To the rear, stairs led to a second-story balcony opening onto a hallway, the balcony railing draped with a smaller Navajo rug.

Katy turned, not realizing until that moment that one wall of sparkling glass framed a magnificent view of Mt. Shasta. The massive peak, snow-covered and serene, rose between a cut in the closer, less spectacular mountains, its breathtaking beauty soaring beyond the glory of any man-made creation. A scarf of windswept cloud clung to the glistening peak, the snow now tinted a rosy pink sculpted with violet shadows in the slanting rays of the setting sun.

She looked around again with a vague feeling of astonishment. This morning she was a woman without an identity, her only possessions a hospital-issue toothbrush and the clothes donated by Dr. Fischer. Now she had a name, an identity, a home! And soon it would *feel* like home, she vowed with sudden fierceness. Soon she'd remember everything.

She jumped as something landed in her lap. The cat, boldly planting its forelegs on her chest, stared into her face with jewel blue eyes. Its fur was marked like a Siamese, silvery tan with darker points, but it had a mere button of a tail. A moment later another cat joined the stare down, this one orange, with golden eyes gleaming and long tail twitching. Do I like cats? Katy wondered, momentarily uncertain.

"Maggie and Tillie! You naughty girls!" Mrs. L. sailed in from the kitchen and swooped up the cats, one under each arm. "You know you're not supposed to be in this part of the house." The big cats, obviously not intimidated by the scolding, merely purred complacently.

"It's okay. I like cats," Katy said. Yes, she did, she thought with a pleased sense of discovery. She liked cats.

"You do?" Mrs. L. hesitated. "Well, yes, of course you do!"

The cats had their 9 Lives, and Katy ate the homemade chicken soup Mrs. L. speed-thawed in the microwave, along with grilled-cheese sandwiches and hot chocolate. Her favorites when she was a girl, Mrs. L. reminded her. Comfort food. Katy smiled to herself. Definitely no den of iniquity here. Afterward Mrs. L. led her to the master bedroom opening off a hallway tucked behind the stairs to the balcony.

"You always stayed in a room upstairs when you came to visit before Thornton and Mavis's accident, but this last time you took over the master bedroom. It's much larger, of course."

Did she detect a faint note of disapproval in Mrs. L.'s voice? Katy wondered. Actually, peering at the room that was homey

33

and cozy in spite of its size, she did feel as if she were intruding on the privacy of strangers. The furniture was charmingly mismatched, as if each piece had been lovingly chosen: antique trunk as a nightstand on one side of the gleaming brass bed, round table covered with a ruffled pink cloth on the other. Wicker chairs by the window, a roll-top oak desk, and a big cherry chest of drawers. A faint, pleasantly lemony scent of furniture polish hung over all. The only discordant note was a long, dark stain on the carpet, as if something had splashed there. Katy stopped short. Blood?

Mrs. L. read Katy's shocked first impression. "Wine, I think. I never could get it out," she said apologetically.

Katy hadn't much choice about where to sleep, even if Mrs. L. disapproved; she couldn't navigate the stairs to the second-floor bedrooms with her crutches. Then she noticed all the boxes and cartons stacked near the chest of drawers.

"What's all this?"

"Before you left, you asked me to contact your roommates in New York and tell them you wouldn't be back and to ship all your things out here. There's also a stack of mail," Mrs. L. added, gesturing to piles on both the desk and the chest of drawers.

"I was giving up modeling?"

"I don't know, sweetie. That was one of the things you wanted to go off somewhere and think about, I guess."

Katy assumed she'd have some insight into her own thought processes eventually, but at the moment this decision about getting away to think simply bewildered her. After New York, wouldn't the isolated ranch be the perfect getaway spot for thinking? Why go somewhere else?

"Mrs. L., do I seem different to you?"

"Why, uh, no, I don't think so, sweetie. Why do you ask that?"

"Dr. Fischer said she'd read that amnesia can cause minor, sometimes even major, personality changes, and everything I hear about myself just seems so...strange and foreign."

"Maybe you are a little different in some ways," Mrs. L. conceded, "but you're still *you*. Sweetie, while we're on this subject there's something I wanted to mention to you." Mrs. L., as if uncomfortable with this subject, twisted the pocket on the flowered apron she'd tied over her polyester pants. "I think it would be best if you didn't mention anything to people about this little memory problem."

The advice startled Katy. She didn't see how she could avoid the subject of her "little memory problem." "People are surely going to know something's wrong when I can't remember them or anything that's happened! Why not just tell the truth?"

"People will probably never even notice, if you're careful. Your folks moved out here after you'd started your modeling career in New York, and you've only been here a few times, so people don't really know you. If something awkward comes up you can just pass it off as, oh, a little minor forgetfulness or strain from your accident. A car accident, you can call it. I hate to say this about people, but they can be so unkind, even prejudiced, about mental...irregularities." Mrs. L. shook her head and patted Katy's arm a little helplessly. "I had an aunt who was in a mental institution for a while, and after she got out some people avoided her as if they thought her problems were catching. I just don't want you to be hurt."

How well Katy remembered Stanton Riker's attitude that her loss of memory signified other mental shortcomings, plus his obvious distaste with her general situation. She didn't like to be less than up front about this; she somehow felt that she was basically an honest person. But perhaps in this instance... She finally nodded slowly. "Although, from the looks of things, I won't be seeing much of anyone anyway. We're not exactly a center of social activity here, are we?"

Mrs. L. smiled. "That's true. But there are people around, some of whom seem to think it's their sworn duty to spread gossip. The postmistress in Wilding, and the people who run the little store there, the Carltons. Old Joe Barnes, the handyman over at the Boys Ranch, who helps me out occasionally. Although I don't mean to say *he's* a gossip, just a little nosy in a friendly sort of way. It might be best if your roommates back in New York didn't know either, in case you decide to go back to modeling. You've complained about how catty and competitive everyone in the business is. It might somehow wind up being used against you." The faint lines between Mrs. L.'s good-hearted blue eyes deepened with worried concern.

Katy squeezed her hand. "It'll be our secret. Hopefully it won't be long before I'm remembering everything anyway."

"The doctor said you might never remember."

"But I'm going to," Katy stated firmly. Although, at this point, she had to admit that statement was more hope than rooted belief.

Mrs. L. turned back the covers on the bed. The sheets were a lovely soft cream, patterned with tiny flowers, the spread an old-fashioned quilt with a design of interlocking rings. She picked up the phone from the table by the bed, checking to be certain it was working. "There's no intercom system because your father thought they were rude, but if you'll leave the door open, I can hear if you call for me."

"I'll be fine."

She was. She had evidently already removed her parents' things from the walk-in closet, and it held only some casual pants and sweaters, plus a burgundy robe and a short, silky black nightie.

She undressed and slipped into the skimpy garment, laughing when she spied herself in the full length mirror on the closet door. Glamorous she was not, with the awkward cast sticking out from under the silky material and her hair closer to bowling-ball smooth than shampoo-ad lush. Actually, she thought uncomfortably as she tried to stretch the skimpy fabric to cover a bit more exposed skin, she didn't really feel like a glamorous-nightie person. More a flannel-pajamas type. Which was perhaps one of those little personality changes Dr. Fischer had mentioned.

She was curious about the contents of the boxes and the stack of mail but too tired tonight to investigate. She simply took a sponge bath in the big bathroom, where pink dolphins danced on the shower curtain, brushed her teeth with the familiar hospital toothbrush, slid into bed, and fell instantly into dreamless sleep.

In the morning she woke to the tempting smells of coffee perking and bacon frying. She dressed in underthings she found in a drawer, a sweater from the closet, and her slit-legged jeans, reluctant to ruin a pair of the expensive, slim-legged pants in the closet. She clumped out to the kitchen, where a radio blared a cheerful country and western song and the cats purred from their perches snuggled between more green plants in the sunny windowsill of the breakfast nook. Mrs. L. stood by a calendar tacked to the wall, hands on hips, a frown on her face.

"Will you look at that? I completely forgot. I have a den-tist's appointment in Yreka this morning! I'll have to call and cancel—"

"Oh, no need to do that," Katy assured her. "I can manage by myself for a few hours."

"But—"

"And while you're in town, perhaps you could pick up

some pajamas for me? Just plain cotton ones. This evening we'll go into the financial situation and see about getting a check off to the hospital and your money returned to you."

Mrs. L. tapped her jaw on the lower left side. "Well, if you really don't mind staying alone. I hate to drive into town again, but this tooth has been nagging at me."

"Maggie and Tillie and I will be fine, won't we, cats?"

Mrs. L. served Katy's breakfast and fussed over showing her what was in the refrigerator for lunch before hurrying out to the car. Katy lingered over coffee after she was alone, feeling as purry and relaxed as the cats in the spring sunshine. Finally, with her curiosity fueled by the hearty breakfast and morning energy, she went back to the bedroom, cats tagging along, and started opening the stacked cartons.

Her roommates, who were as lost to her memory as everything else, were not the greatest packers, she decided with a certain annoyance. The clothes looked as if they'd simply been yanked off hangers and jammed into the boxes. The high heel of a silvery sandal snagged the sleeve of an expensive angora sweater, and a belt wound like a leather snake around a tangled lump of pantyhose. Carelessly tossed-in makeup had leaked and ruined a silk blouse.

The first two boxes were easy to get to, but the others were stacked higher. Was there anything breakable in them, or could she just shove the top one to the floor where she could get at it? Shove, she decided, and did so.

Except that at the same moment she shoved, Maggie crouched to leap for the box. Katy tried to stop the box from falling on the cat...stumbled into the big chest of drawers...thumped her cast down on the other cat's tail...felt the chest of drawers wobble as she clutched it to keep from falling.... And the next thing she knew she was in an avalanche of falling cartons, tumbling chest of drawers, flying photos, and mail, the entire disaster punctuated by clawing, screeching cats.

Then she was on the floor, boxes around her like fallen monuments and cast-bound leg trapped under the chest of drawers. The cats eyed her reproachfully from the safety of the bed.

"Well, of all the dumb, clumsy...and I'm talking to you, cats, not just to myself," she muttered.

She raised up on her elbows to assess the situation and immediately got jabbed in the middle by a carved corner of the chest of drawers. She was on her back with the heavy chest crunched down on the cast. Broken glass from a framed photo, a photo of herself, stabbed the carpet beside her head. She gingerly tossed the glass aside and checked for damages and injuries, wiggling toes and fingers and cautiously exploring scalp for reopened wounds. Except for a cat-scratched arm and a crampy feeling in her injured right hand, everything seemed fine; no serious damages.

But there *was* one slight problem. She couldn't move.

Ridiculous. Of course she could move. All she had to do was wiggle out from under this awkward weight—

She wiggled. She squirmed. She twisted, pushed, and pulled. She panted and rested and struggled again.

No use. She couldn't reach the cast to move it with her hands, and she couldn't lift the chest. She couldn't even sit up, with the corner of the heavy chest poking her middle every time she tried. An odd scratching noise outside the window suddenly made her stiffen. Something...*someone?*...trying to get in? And she was trapped here, helpless—

Just a rose bush brushing against the house, she realized, feeling foolish about the instant panic. She commanded her rigid spine and clenched fists to relax. She might be flat on her back, even trapped, but there was nothing to be afraid of. Mrs.

L. had lived here alone for months. After a few more moments, the faint sound ceased.

Her tense awareness did not.

Now there was only the silence, an oddly disturbing, even eerie silence. The cats were gone, quietly vanished, the intricate design of the bedspread different from this point of view, something oddly menacing about the labyrinth of interlocked rings, like a maze from which there was no exit. No song or chatter of birds outside, no quiet hum of household appliances quietly going about their everyday business. It was like a moment suspended in time…and with it came a strange, disturbing feeling that everything here was wrong, *all wrong,* that somehow it was all a complicated illusion, a stage set. Her parents were dead, her memory in limbo. If someone wanted *her* dead all they had to do was walk in now and here she was, trapped and helpless—

She shivered, body taut as an arched bow, gaze riveted on the doorway, ears straining.

Then Tillie peered in the doorway, meowed, and the strangeness whooshed out of the moment like water spiraling down a drain. For a woman with an undersupply of memory, she scolded herself, she definitely had an *over*supply of imagination.

Okay, she was indeed a bit uncomfortable lying here on the floor helpless as an overturned bug, but she was in no real danger. She could just read her mail until Mrs. L. got home. She craned her head to look at the clock on the antique trunk and groaned. Only nine o'clock. Given the long drive to and from Yreka, plus Mrs. L.'s dental appointment and shopping time, she could be trapped here for another five or six *hours.*

There was the phone, if she could somehow reach it. But who would she call? She doubted the existence of quick help from 911 out here in the wilds. Oh, but there was the handyman from the boys ranch across the road— What was his name? Joe. Yes, she'd call Joe.

The phone was out of reach, but she tossed a picture frame at it and the receiver tumbled to the floor. She bent a metal hanger into a long, narrow shape and snagged the receiver with it. Then, a piece of luck! The number of the boys ranch, along with several other numbers, was taped right to the phone. She held the instrument overhead and punched in the numbers from her awkward position on the floor.

On the third ring a male voice answered. "Damascus Boys Ranch. Jace Foster speaking."

"Hi. Is Joe the handyman available?"

"I'm sorry. Joe went to town for supplies today. May I help you?"

The husky voice sounded authoritative but nice, cheerful and neighborly, the offer of help more genuine than mere polite phone etiquette. Where she hadn't liked Stanton Riker on sight, she liked Jace Foster simply from his friendly voice.

She started to say, *You don't know me,* but stopped. Maybe they did know each other. She detoured that tricky obstacle by jumping right in with her problem. "Hi. This is Katy Cavanaugh from across the road. I hate to bother you, but I've gotten myself in a rather ridiculous fix here—"

She broke off sharply. He hadn't said a word, made no response at all, and yet she felt the oddest sensation, as if the very phone lines prickled. The fine hairs on her arm prickled in response, and she swallowed convulsively. There was her imagination in overdrive again. Determinedly she set the peculiar feeling aside and started over. "I was opening some cartons, you see, and—"

"Kat?" he interrupted. *"Kat?"* He sounded not just surprised, she thought, but incredulous.

Apparently they did know each other, although he certainly

did not sound overjoyed to hear from her. She thought about explaining that she used the name Katy rather than Kat now, but at the moment, that detail seemed irrelevant. The chest of drawers on her leg was getting heavier by the moment. "Yes, Kat Cavanaugh. I'm really sorry to bother you but—"

"Is this some kind of trick?" he demanded.

"Trick?" she repeated, taken aback by the odd question that sounded more like an accusation. *Nice* and *neighborly* had definitely vanished from his voice. So much for judging character by phone-answering technique, she thought wryly. "No, of course not!"

"Are you…here?"

"Mrs. L. came for me, and we arrived last night. My leg is broken and in a cast. I was unpacking some things in the bedroom a few minutes ago and accidentally knocked over a chest of drawers, and now the cast is trapped under it. Mrs. Lennox is gone and won't be back for several hours, so I was just wondering if someone could come over and lend me a hand—"

Again that peculiar, penetrating silence. Katy felt mildly indignant. Weren't Christians supposed to be helpful and nice? Jace Foster appeared in no rush to be either. In spite of the fact that the trapped leg was beginning to ache, a quicksilver shiver of apprehension rippled through her, and she had a quick impulse simply to hang up.

Too late.

"Okay, I'll be right over."

"Don't—" She didn't get the remainder of the *Don't bother* out before he broke the connection, now giving an impression of sudden haste.

She replaced the receiver with the uneasy feeling that the phone call had been a big mistake. Something was definitely odd here. Yet he had seemed so *pleasant* at first.…

Until he found out who she was.

Now what did *that* say?

She briefly comforted herself with the thought that perhaps he wouldn't come after all. He'd sounded more astonished and resentful than concerned about her predicament. But in less than five minutes a vehicle roared into the driveway. A moment later the front door opened.

"Kat?" The sound of the tense male voice erased a tiny hope that the vehicle might be Mrs. L. returning early.

Her fingers dug into the carpet as her apprehension climbed like a panicked cat scrambling up a tree. This was no eerie, imagined moment of irrational fear. This was real. She was trapped, vulnerable, flat-on-her-back helpless. And she'd blithely informed a total stranger of this. She jammed a knuckle against her mouth. She wouldn't respond to his call. Maybe he'd go away—

No, not going away.

Footsteps crossed the polished hardwood floor of the living room. A spot in the floor beside the staircase creaked. And then a tanned hand and muscular arm shoved the bedroom door open wide.

Four

He hesitated, then strode across the room to stare down at her. He loomed over her, legs impossibly long, fisted hands heavy and dangerous, shoulders broad enough to fill the room and block the ceiling. She felt like some wild creature, trapped and helpless in the dark headlights of his hostile gaze, that strange prickle she'd felt on the phone line a skeletal finger jabbing her spine now. If she were not already pinned to the floor, his hostile eyes would have done it.

She fought a frantic urge to close her eyes like a frightened child and pretend he wasn't there. Even in those first dazed days in the hospital she had never felt so alone, so helplessly vulnerable.

Desperately she tried to bluff an air of self-confidence, as if this were an ordinary conversation between two equals. "I'm sorry I had to bother you." But her voice couldn't manage the pretense. Her breathing was too shallow, air barely reaching her lungs. The words wobbled out in a stammer when she got to, "Th-thank you for coming."

"What happened to you?" he demanded without prelimi-naries.

"I told you, I was unpacking cartons, and I accidentally knocked over the chest of drawers—"

"No, I mean, *this*." His rough slash of hand took in every-thing from her shorn head to her sock-covered foot sticking out of the cast. Then, as if coming to the tardy realization that this was no time to stand there demanding explanations, he muttered, "Never mind."

He knelt and leaned over her to plant a two-handed grip on the chest, and with her hands and good foot she propelled herself backwards in a scooting crab-walk as soon as the cast was free. He manhandled the chest of drawers to a standing position with a single masculine grunt and slammed shut the drawers that had slid open. With a few swift gestures he gathered up the fallen mail and photos and several pieces of broken glass.

"I wouldn't walk around barefoot in here," he advised. "There could still be slivers of glass in the carpet." He skirted the dark stain on the carpet as he crossed the room to a wicker wastebasket.

Katy, feeling she wouldn't be quite so vulnerable if she were on her feet, grabbed a brass leg of the bed and levered herself upright.

He wasn't quite as oversized as he had appeared from her flat-on-the-floor position staring up at him, but his brawny size was still intimidating. At least six foot two, probably a hundred and ninety pounds of lean, lick-his-weight-in-wildcats muscle, a square jaw that shouted *stubborn*, thick brown hair. The green-gold glints in his hazel eyes offered no more warmth than had his voice on the phone, but at the moment his expression also appeared more reluctantly curious than menacing.

"You okay?" he asked.

"Yes, I'm fine." She wasn't positive of that, but she didn't want him lingering to investigate. She ran her free hand over her scalp, wondering if in the past running her fingers through her hair had been some automatic reaction to a nerve-frizzing situation. "I appreciate your coming. I can manage by myself now."

"Did the cast crack or break? You should probably see a doctor for x-rays—"

He took a step toward her, as if he planned to inspect the

46

cast himself, and hastily she said, "Yes, I'll see about that as soon as Mrs. L. gets home." Anything to get rid of him. She felt as unsteady as a wind chime in a storm and desperately wanted to sit down, but she wasn't about to reveal any further weakness by collapsing in front of him. She clutched the brass rail at the foot of the bed and determinedly remained on her feet. Foot.

But he wasn't going yet. He hooked his hands in the pockets of his khaki pants and eyed her appraisingly. "What *did* happen to you?"

"I was in an....accident." She couldn't bring herself to use the phony car accident that Mrs. L. had suggested, but "accident" alone was relatively accurate without being overly revealing. "The doctor had to cut my hair in order to suture the scalp wounds. And my leg, of course, is broken."

"Have you made a decision about the ranch?"

"Decision?" she faltered again. What decision?

"My offer is still open."

He sounded as if he were expecting some specific response to that statement, perhaps even challenging her to make that response. She simply felt confused. Was he saying she'd been thinking about selling the ranch, and he'd offered to buy it? The treacherous potholes of this conversation were suddenly too much for her; she was too exhausted to cope with them. Without knowing exactly how she'd gotten there, she also realized she was now slumped on the edge of the bed after all.

For a moment she was tempted to blurt out, *I don't know you, and I have no idea what you're talking about!* But instead she said lamely, "Well, uh, thank you. I'll think about your offer." Perhaps Mrs. L. would know what this was about.

He crossed to the bed in three long strides, strong hand on her shoulder, steadying her as if he thought she might crumple to the floor. "Are you sure you're okay?"

"Yes. I just feel a little woozy occasionally since the accident."

"Can I get you something? Glass of water? Medication?"

He sounded concerned but reluctantly so, in the same way that he was reluctantly curious about her injuries. She wanted to say simply, *No, go away!* But her mouth did feel cottony dry.

"Yes, I'd appreciate a glass of water, please."

He turned, saw the open bathroom door, and headed there rather than the kitchen. His muscular silhouette filled the doorway when he went through, the paper cup from the bathroom dispenser looking absurdly tiny and fragile in his hand when he returned.

"Thank you." She gulped a swallow of water, her wary eyes never leaving his face. As if aware of her uneasiness he stepped back and folded his arms. He apparently wasn't planning to take advantage of her vulnerable situation. She finished the water in two thirsty swallows, and he took the empty cup and tossed it in the wastebasket with the shards of glass.

"Thank you," she repeated.

Her breathing was almost back to normal now, and she was reluctantly curious about him. Beyond the name, Jace Foster, who was he? Why the hostility and air of wary suspicion? Yet, without giving away the peculiarities of her own "little memory problem," she could hardly start firing questions at him. Her first frightened fixation on his size had distracted her from the observation that he was a good-looking man, with strong, clean-cut features, age perhaps thirty or so. A slight, crooked jog in the line of his nose, as if it had perhaps been broken at some time in the past, somehow only added an attractive ruggedness to his good looks. Sun-crinkles creased the tan around his eyes, as if he did not spend all his time in an office, and his hands looked weathered and competent. Again, more questions to ask Mrs. L.

"I'll be okay now," she said. "Thanks again for coming."

He acknowledged the thanks with a noncommittal nod. He seemed oddly reluctant to leave in spite of her polite dismissal. The fact that she was uncertain whether this was concern for her physical condition, curiosity, or something more sinister brought another wave of uneasiness.

"Why did you change from the name you've always used, Kat, to Katy?" he asked unexpectedly.

"I'm not sure." She smiled, trying to defuse the hostility that still crackled like a high-voltage wire loose in the room. "I guess I just thought it went better with the new hairdo."

"That's a hairdo?" For a moment he sounded almost teasing, as if he were on the verge of a sun ray of smile himself, and for an equally brief moment the unlikely wish that she *could* make him smile flitted through her.

"It cuts down considerably on blow-dry time."

He almost laughed, but instead frowned slightly. "You seem...different," he said. His eyes appraised her again, like someone suspiciously peering into the magician's hat to find the trick behind the rabbit. Then his gaze shifted to the photo of her he'd propped on the chest of drawers. Comparing them? Knowing she was an impostor?

But I'm not an impostor! she silently corrected herself instantly. *I'm Kat. Katy. Kathryn Anne Cavanaugh.* And she did not want to get into any discussion about *differentness.* She didn't even think before, still trying to distract him, she said lightly, "Maybe it's the hair again. Maybe, like Samson, I lost all my power when it was shorn."

That statement obviously surprised him. He came close to doing a sitcom double take. But it certainly didn't surprise him any more than it did her. What did she know of Samson or any other biblical character? How did she even know Samson *was* a man from the Bible?

He apparently decided not to ask that question, however, merely shrugging to dismiss the subject of her missing hair. "Yeah, maybe so."

"Thanks again."

"Sure. Tell Mrs. Lennox that Joe was going to pick up a new filter for her car today and he'll be over to change the oil for her later."

"I'll tell her. Thank you."

Her gaze followed his exit, her heart flipping nervously when he paused at the door to look back at her. For a moment she thought he was going to stalk back and…do what? But, after a moment of standing in the doorway with another faint frown, he went on. She heard a reverse of the noises he'd made when arriving: squeak of floor by the stairs, front door opening, roar of engine. When she was sure he was gone, she let herself collapse sideways on the bed.

A strange encounter, she reflected as she lay there slowly regrouping both mentally and physically. Strange and disturbing. The odd way he kept studying her, the hostility, the feeling that there was more here than showed on the surface.

Yet when Mrs. L. returned home and began answering questions, Katy had to admit there was reason for Jace Foster's hostility.

Five

They were in the kitchen, Katy delighted with the flower-trimmed, floppy-brimmed hat Mrs. L. had brought her in addition to the new cotton pajamas. She slipped it on her head and struck a coquettish pose.

"I feel very Southern belle-ish," she said.

Mrs. L. smiled, obviously pleased that Katy liked the little surprise. "Good. Because we're having Southern fried chicken tonight."

Katy knew she was going to get a scolding when Mrs. L. learned about the accident, and she sat there fidgeting with a ribbon flowing from the hat while she tried to figure how to ask questions about her visitor without revealing why he'd come to the house.

Finally she said with careful casualness, "A man from across the road dropped in for a few minutes while you were gone."

Mrs. L., standing on a kitchen step stool to put groceries away, shoved a carton of oatmeal into an upper cupboard. "Joe?"

"No. His name was Jace Foster, although he said Joe would be over later to change the oil in your car."

Mrs. L. turned so suddenly on the stool that she had to grab a cabinet door to catch her balance. "Jace came over here?" She sounded almost as surprised as Jace had by Katy's phone call. "Why?"

"It's unusual for him to come here?" He'd seemed to know his way around the house.

"He used to come over fairly often, but now—I can't imagine him just *dropping in* on you."

"Actually," Katy admitted reluctantly, "I had to call for help, and he was the one who came."

"*Help?*"

Then Katy had to tell the whole story about her minor disaster, and she did get scolded for her carelessness.

"Why, you might have smashed the cast and broken your leg again! After this I'm not leaving unless I can find someone to stay with you!"

"I don't need a baby-sitter," Katy grumbled, although today hadn't offered much proof of that. "I'm fine."

But Mrs. L. went over the cast like a NASA inspector searching a space rocket for microscopic flaws. She Band-Aided the cat scratch, inspected Katy's scalp, and would have bundled her into the car for an instant trip to the doctor until Katy persuaded her that with no pain and the cast intact it was unlikely there was a problem with the leg.

Finally, after all that, as Mrs. L. calmed her nerves with a cup of chamomile tea, Katy had a chance to ask the questions that had led her to admit to the accident. First, exactly who was Jace Foster?

"I suppose his title is manager or supervisor or something like that. He started the boys ranch a year or two before we came here. He was a professional football player before that."

"Do you know him very well?"

"He was Thornton and Mavis's friend, of course, and I've only talked to him a few times since their deaths. But I see him taking the boys on hikes or horseback riding, sometimes playing ball or working in the garden or building fence with them."

"Is he married?" Now why had she asked *that* question, Katy wondered, annoyed with herself.

"No. I think Damascus is his life. I know your parents

thought very highly of him and his work with the boys. They were planning to donate forty acres of this place to add to the school grounds."

That information startled Katy, although she supposed it shouldn't have, given what Mrs. L. had said earlier about her parents' generous nature. "Did Jace Foster know they planned to do that?"

"Oh, yes. It had already been surveyed. The stakes and ribbons are still out there in the woods. Of course I understand why *you* wouldn't want to do it," Mrs. L. added.

"You mean I backed out of an agreement my parents had made?" Katy felt a stirring of dismay.

"Nothing had actually been signed before they died, so you are certainly within your rights to do what you want with the property."

"Why didn't I want to go through with the donation?"

"You were talking about selling the ranch for use as a fishing resort or dude ranch. The larger acreage would be worth a lot more money, especially with the most usable river frontage being on the forty acres they were going to donate to Damascus."

Katy nodded slowly as the course of events became clear. "And then Jace made an offer on the ranch, and I turned it down."

"Yes, I believe so."

Okay, Jace probably had a right to be disappointed, Katy granted. But it was apparently a simple business decision on her part, nothing he should be so *hostile* about.

A little hesitantly Mrs. L. added, "Then there was also the matter of letting the boys cross the land and use the river." Katy had only her usual blank ignorance in response to that statement, and Mrs. L. went on with an explanation. "Most of the river in this area is very wild and dangerous, but there's one nice, wide, slow-moving spot that Thornton and Mavis always let Jace and the boys use for swimming and kayaking. But you decided they couldn't cross the ranch or use the river anymore. Joe said you told Jace that if he or any of the boys came on the property again, you'd have them charged with trespassing."

"Why did I do that?" Katy felt bewildered. It seemed like such a petty, *mean* thing to do to the disadvantaged boys.

"Maybe you thought they'd damage or steal something, perhaps devalue the property in some way."

Later that day, Mrs. L. brought out an armload of photo albums, and they went through them together. Katy knew the fact that none of the photos roused even a faint twinge of recognition for her frustrated Mrs. L., and she tried very hard to absorb the past they represented. Even if she couldn't remember it, she could *learn* that past and make it a part of herself. Yet thoughts of Jace kept simmering in the back of her mind, and even as Mrs. L. was showing her a photo of a school play, telling how Katy played a boy's part because she was taller than everyone, she was thinking about Jace and her banning of his boys from the river.

Yes, plenty of reason for his hostility, she had to admit. Yet she almost felt there was something more.

Katy suddenly interrupted the story of the school play. "Mrs. L., was there something else between Jace and me? Something other than business dealings?"

Mrs. L. turned a page of the photo album slowly. "Possibly. You saw quite a lot of him before the disagreements about the property."

Katy tapped her fingers on the hard surface of the cast as she uneasily considered the disturbing possibilities of that relationship. The *not knowing* about everything that had gone on before these last few weeks of her life made her feel so helpless, as if she were an outsider peering in and everyone knew secrets she didn't. Her head suddenly swam and ached with the futile effort of trying to remember anything about the photos in the stacks of albums. She abandoned the project with the excuse that she wanted to take the daily nap Dr. Fischer had advised.

She didn't think she'd sleep, with her mind churning restlessly, but she did, and she felt better when she woke. Joe arrived just as they were finishing dinner, knocking on the back door rather than coming to the front. After he changed the oil and filter in the Honda, Mrs. L. let him wash up in the laundry room and then invited him in for coffee and cookies. He looked uneasy when he saw Katy sitting in the breakfast nook. He tipped the bill of his cap politely, however, obviously trying not to stare at her new "hairdo." He didn't sit, instead stood at the counter, where Mrs. L. set coffee and peanut-butter cookies in front of him. With his lanky, almost bony build, he obviously didn't have to worry about weight, and he immediately downed three big cookies. He was about Mrs. L.'s age, Katy guessed, but considerably more weathered.

"Kat…Katy was in an accident, in case you haven't heard," Mrs. L. said. "So she's come back here to stay for a while now."

Joe's neutral response, "That's too bad," left Katy wryly wondering if the "too bad" meant the accident or her being here at the ranch. Had she also been unpleasant to him? she wondered, or did she simply share Jace's hostility about the ranch? Winning friends and influencing people apparently was not a strong point of her character.

She finished her own coffee and excused herself, suspecting that both Joe and Mrs. L. would be more comfortable without her presence. She was right, she decided, when the conversation picked up even before she reached the arched doorway to the dining room. Joe was saying something about how he'd spotted Mrs. L. in town at a corner phone booth and he'd wanted to take her to lunch, but she was gone before he could find a parking space in the next block. She could hear the two of them laughing companionably together while she watched the news on TV. On impulse, when she heard him getting ready to leave, she clumped back to the kitchen.

"Joe, could you tell Mr. Foster something for me?"

"I reckon." He eyed her warily, as if he suspected some barrage of complaints or criticism.

"I have no objection to his taking the boys across this place and using the river, so they're welcome to do that again if they'd like."

"Yeah, I'll tell him." Joe's watery blue eyes lit up. "He'll be real glad to hear it, especially now that the weather's warming up."

Tired of the slit pantsleg flapping around the cast, the first thing Katy did the following morning was whack it off at the thigh. Dr. Fischer called a few minutes later with the name of a doctor in Yreka for Katy to see.

"A head doctor or a broken-bones doctor?" Katy teased lightly.

"Broken bones. But if you want the other kind, I'll dig up a name for you."

"No, I'll wait for nature to take its course." She hesitated and then added, "If it wouldn't be a violation of medical ethics, could you not mention my amnesia when you send my records down to Dr. Ralston? Mrs. L. and I decided it would be better if just the two of us know."

"No reason the other doctor needs to know." Dr. Fischer agreed. But the question apparently prompted her to ask, "Are you sure you're really getting along okay?"

Katy decided not to worry her with yesterday's mishap. "Doing great, and Mrs. L. is wonderful. I'm going to ride in to Wilding to pick up the mail with her a little later. This is a beautiful place, with a spectacular view of Mt. Shasta."

"Bringing back memories?"

Katy sighed. "Not a one. But Mrs. L. is giving me a crash course in the life and times of Kat Cavanaugh, so maybe something will ring a bell eventually."

"Hang in there. It will come. And Katy, call me after you've seen the doctor, okay? Call me anytime, in fact, if you just want to talk."

"Thanks. I will."

She called the doctor's office and made an appointment for the following week. She remembered then that she and Mrs. L. hadn't gotten around to dealing with the financial situation yet, and she should write a check to send to the hospital before they went to the post office. She was just heading for the desk in the bedroom when a snatch of a rowdy, old rock-and-roll song flooded the room. It took her a moment to realize that it was the doorbell, and, also realizing this was something her inventive father must have done, she went to the door with a smile of amusement on her face. Cornball, yes, but sweet.

She cut off the smile when she opened the door and saw the rugged, unsmiling figure standing there. He was in heavy, dark work pants today, cowboy-style straw hat in one hand, leather work gloves tucked in a rear pocket. A pleasant scent of pine clung to him. He brushed at a scattering of broken pine needles clinging to his plaid shirt.

"I've been cutting wood with a couple of the boys." Jace

stopped speaking for a moment. "Joe said you'd changed your mind about prohibiting us from crossing your property and using the river."

"Yes." She didn't elaborate further because she didn't know why she'd enacted the ban in the first place.

"Thank you. I appreciate that." He tapped the hat against his lean, muscled leg. "Would you mind putting it in writing?"

She blinked, taken aback by the blunt request. She hadn't expected effusive gratitude, but neither had she expected this distrustful response. "You mean a legal document, notarized and everything?"

He shuffled his booted feet uncomfortably, and she thought she also detected a faint hint of embarrassed color rising under the tan. "Well, no, just a written statement will do." Then, as if he suddenly felt guilty about making the unfriendly request, he withdrew it. "But I suppose that isn't necessary. It's just that, after you threatened—Never mind, forget it. Thanks again for changing your mind." He turned away from the door.

"No, no, come in. I'll be glad to put it in writing." She swung the door open wide in a determined display of hospitality, and managed to throw herself off balance and lose a crutch in the process. She would have tumbled to the floor if he hadn't caught her.

He tilted her upright. Flustered and annoyingly near tears, she tried to make light of the situation.

"I seem as tippy as a beginning tightrope walker, don't I? First yesterday and now this. I'll just go find pen and paper—"

She tried to move away but he didn't release her. Instead his arm clamped tighter, his expression puzzled as he looked down at her. *You seem different,* he'd said yesterday. His hazel eyes repeated that statement now. Up close, she knew he must also be seeing the fresh scars that were not yet, as Dr. Fischer had assured her they eventually would be, hidden by her hair.

"Looks as if you had a real collision with something."

"Yes."

"Did this happen back in New York?"

"No. It was up in Oregon." She broke off, thinking she shouldn't have said that because it opened the door on more questions. She was right; he instantly jumped on the statement.

"Oregon? What were you doing there? How did you get there?"

It was on her tongue to say, *I have no idea how I got to Oregon or what I was doing there!* But she caught herself and simply repeated what Mrs. L. had told her. "I just needed some time and space to think. If you could just hand me my other crutch...."

He kept one hand on her arm while he snagged the crutch with his foot. He helped her position the crutch under her arm and made certain she was balanced before he let go, seeming reluctant to do so even then. She hobbled to an end table where she'd seen a pad of paper and scrawled an authorization for Jace Foster and/or anyone from the Damascus Boys Ranch to cross her property and use the river at any time, such permission to be in effect until rescinded in writing.

"About the other, the sale or donation of the land..." She saw him tense as if expecting a confrontation. "I don't feel in a position to make a decision at the moment, but I'll give it more thought."

He looked surprised but didn't comment. He glanced briefly at the paper she handed him before placing it in his shirt pocket. "Thank you." He hesitated and then, with an odd blend of truce and challenge in his voice, muttered, "Maybe the world would be a better place if more people got bumped on the head. It seems to have made a big improvement in you."

It was a backhanded compliment at best. "Now if someone would just give *you* a good whack!" she retorted.

His slow, embarrassed smile grudgingly admitted that he could perhaps use a bit of personality adjustment himself. The smile did something totally unexpected to Katy, and a feeling like melted butter flowed through her in a warm, golden flood. They looked at each other with mutually guilty grins.

But, as if some unpleasant memory suddenly jabbed him, the smile flattened, and he raked his fingers through his dark hair. Finally he said, "Would you like to come along and watch the boys with their inflatable kayaks tomorrow afternoon? I could take you back to the river in the pickup."

In spite of the shared grins, the offer did not come with the warmth of old friends making up after a spat. In fact, there was a definite lack of enthusiasm, as if Jace's better judgment collided with a sense of obligation to make the offer as thanks for her change of mind. It was enough to congeal that golden flow within her to a greasy puddle.

She started to decline, then, almost perversely, because she suspected he'd rather she refused, she lifted her chin with a defiant toss. "Yes, I think I'd like that."

Six

After Jace left, Katy searched the rolltop desk in the bedroom for a checkbook. She couldn't find a current one, which didn't surprise her; she'd probably taken it with her when she left the ranch and lost it along with her other identification. She did find fresh pads of checks, however, from a bank in New York and a money market account at a Redding bank. She started opening the various bank and credit card statements that had accumulated in her absence.

The New York account was minimal, but the money market balance was large enough to make her blink. Yes, she could easily pay the hospital's bill. She didn't fully understand the complicated statements from a stockbroker in San Francisco, but they certainly suggested an impressive total of assets. Statements from VISA and MasterCard showed zero balances.

Then a peculiarity struck her. Earlier statements were thick with canceled checks, but apparently she hadn't written a single check nor made any credit card charges since leaving the ranch. She leafed through the earlier canceled checks and credit card charges that detailed her life in New York, curiosity changing to an appalled fascination: two-hundred-dollar haircuts, massages, facials, waxing, herbal wraps, pedicures, clothes and shoes, a personal trainer, an expensive health club, a drama coach, a limousine service, a photographer.

She was, she thought with chagrin, a very high-maintenance woman.

Almost absentmindedly she traced a fingertip over the signature on a canceled check, the flourish of the K in Kat, the flamboyant loop of the *C* in Cavanaugh. Impulsively she wrote her name across the back of an envelope and slipped it below the check to align the signatures. She frowned, puzzled, at the results.

Mrs. L. tapped on the open door. She'd been outside fertilizing the rose bushes. "Hungry for lunch, sweetie?"

Katy motioned her inside. "Look at this. They don't look anything alike."

Mrs. L. peered over her shoulder. "I'm not surprised, after that injury to your hand. I sprained my right wrist once, and for a month I couldn't put my lipstick on without looking like a clown. Perhaps you should put a bit of Ben-Gay or some other ointment on it."

Katy rubbed her palm, which did indeed still tend to stiffen and cramp occasionally.

Mrs. L. laughed. "In the meantime, you'd better practice getting your signature back to normal, or they'll investigate you for forgery!"

Katy did practice, and by the time she wrote a check to the hospital, her signature was close to her old one, although writing it that way still felt a little awkward. She wrote another check to repay what Mrs. L. had given the hospital, the expenses she'd paid after the household money ran out, and the salary she hadn't received for the months Katy had been away.

Mrs. L. nodded appreciatively when she looked at the generous check. "Thank you. My funds were getting low enough to be worrisome."

Katy thought about that comment as she stamped the envelope addressed to the Benton Beach hospital. Actually, she felt rather indignant about it. What Mrs. L. had spent on the hospital and household expenses had apparently almost exhausted her inheritance from Katy's parents, which meant that the amount they had willed her hadn't been particularly generous.

Didn't a faithful employee of long standing deserve better? Perhaps she could raise Mrs. L.'s salary.

Which reminded her that, even though her financial situation appeared more than adequate at the moment, she must make plans for the future. Which was apparently what she'd gone off to think about some three months ago.

After lunch Katy and Mrs. L. drove to the post office and store that made up the tiny town of Wilding. Coached by Mrs. L., she greeted Mrs. Grantham, the postmistress, and Lea Carlton, the store owner, by name, adding a question Mrs. L. had suggested about Lea's arthritis. Katy's leg cast and "hairdo" drew curiosity and sympathy, and there were no awkward references to the past.

On the way home, as Mrs. L. crowded the shoulder of the road to let a log truck pass, a thought occurred to Katy. "Do I know how to drive?"

"My goodness, until right now it never occurred to me to show you the cars in the garage. And there's your father's workshop you should see, too. I'm sorry," Mrs. L. added apologetically. "I know you can't remember the past, but it slips my own mind that you also don't remember all these little everyday things."

Back at the house, Mrs. L. took Katy on a tour. There were two cars in the garage, a big, solid Buick and a sporty convertible that gleamed like a red jewel even under several months' accumulation of dust.

"Your father loved taking the convertible out for a spin. He'd tell Mavis that he was working because driving it made him feel creative, although we all knew he really just liked to go out and 'play cars.'" Mrs. L. smiled fondly. "Your mother liked to quote that old saying, 'The only difference between men and boys is the price of their toys.'"

Katy smiled and ran her fingers over the sleek surface, leaving faint trails in the dust, almost feeling a contact with her father through this prized possession. "I wonder why I didn't take one of the cars when I left," she mused.

"I don't know, sweetie." Mrs. L. hesitated before adding, "I keep thinking about your being found alone on that beach, and I've wondered if…well, maybe you had some disagreement with your friends and left them and were hitchhiking and got in with the wrong people. I think you had quite a lot of cash with you."

Cash. Yes, that would explain why she hadn't written checks or used her credit cards, and robbery could well have been the motive for what happened to her. But the possibility of hitchhiking astonished Katy. "Would I do that?"

"Maybe. You've always been such an unpredictable free spirit. You didn't know a soul in New York when you took off all alone to get into modeling there."

Unfortunately, Katy thought wryly as she fingered the scar line across her scalp, this latest jaunt had been less successful than her original career move.

Her father's cluttered workshop on the far side of the garage was just as he had left it the day he and Mavis climbed into his private plane for a trip to a conference in Denver, according to Mrs. L. His work still covered the long counters and a central island, everything from ideas in the whimsical drawing stage to half-finished projects that offered little clue to what usage he intended for them. A clever, multilevel bird feeder he'd designed so he could watch the birds while he worked hung outside one window, and purple elephants danced on a wind chime at another window. A big sign on one wall proclaimed "No Batteries!"

"Thornton never invented anything that needed batteries," Mrs. L. explained. "He especially hated battery-operated toys. He said kids should play with things they made work themselves, not just sit and watch a toy do something."

A sweet and playful man, Katy decided, but also wise, and again a pang of loss tangled with guilt and frustration. It seemed such a *betrayal* of her parents not to remember them, a feeling intensified when she started reading one of the children's books her mother had written. She couldn't manage the stairs to her mother's upstairs studio yet, but Mrs. L. brought down an armload of books about an adventurous trio of girls who shared ownership of a horse, and Katy read in bed until almost midnight. Next morning, over fresh-baked cinnamon rolls in the sunny breakfast nook, she asked Mrs. L. about a feeling that still nagged her.

"Do you know of something important I should have done before I left, or perhaps intended to do when I returned? Something connected with my parents, perhaps?"

"Nothing I know of." Mrs. L. gave her a quick, sharp glance. "Are you starting to remember?"

Katy shook her head regretfully. "No, it's just that I keep having this something-unfinished, something-undone feeling, that I've forgotten something very important that I *must* do."

Mrs. L. also shook her head as she wiped the kitchen range. "I'm sure you and the lawyer had Thornton and Mavis's affairs all wrapped up. But there could be various things you intended to do, I suppose. Sell the ranch, perhaps, or embark on a new career? I know you were interested in acting."

Acting. Katy remembered the drama coach among her expenses. Yes, that made sense. Was there some important appointment or contact that prompted this nagging feeling? Then another thought occurred to her. "How do you feel about my selling the ranch, Mrs. L.?"

"I'll miss it, of course. I've loved it here. But I'd also like to be closer to Evan. He's up for promotion and won't be traveling up this way much if he gets it." She smiled, her pride in her son obvious. "Maybe I could ferret out some nice girl for him, since he seems too busy to do it himself. If he isn't working, he's at his health club or out running five or ten miles a day to keep in shape."

Katy smiled at Mrs. L.'s motherly fussiness. "I'd love to see him. Maybe it would stir some of my lost childhood memories. Maybe by then I can even get out and run with him."

"I'll tell him."

Jace hadn't said what time he was taking the boys to the river, but, with a mixture of apprehension and anticipation, Katy parked herself on the front deck right after lunch to be ready when he arrived. Mrs. L., assured that Katy would be in good hands, had left a few minutes earlier to attend her quilting circle at a friend's in Wilding.

Katy had found pink shorts, a scoop-necked T-shirt, and sunglasses in the cartons, and she was also wearing the new hat to protect her exposed scalp. Wearing it as well, she had to admit, because the big, frivolous hat was more flattering than her skimpy "hairdo." Not that she cared how she looked to Jace Foster, of course, but she didn't want to alarm the boys with her strange appearance. When she saw a pickup start down the long driveway of the boys ranch, she picked up her crutches and hobbled down the three steps from the deck, determined to show her self-sufficiency.

Yet when the pickup loaded with paddles and orange life preservers pulled up beside her, she knew she couldn't possibly climb in it alone. She had enough trouble struggling in and out of Mrs. L.'s Honda, and the big pickup was much higher. Oh, this had been a really dumb idea, she muttered silently as Jace came around the pickup to open the door. She was *not* going through the awkwardness of having him push and pull her as if he were trying to load a stranded whale. She'd just tell him she'd changed her mind about going after all.

She didn't get a chance to open her mouth.

In one smooth, seemingly effortless gesture he simply picked her up, supporting the cast with a muscular arm, and deposited her on the pickup seat. He tossed her crutches on top of the life jackets.

"This is really great for the boys," he said, standing inside the open door. He wore faded jeans and old sneakers, baseball cap pushed back on his dark hair, sunglasses hiding his eyes. "I was sorry they got caught in the middle of our…differences."

Again Katy had the odd feeling that their "differences" went beyond problems about the ranch, but the sight of a strange procession turning into the driveway distracted her. "What is *that?*"

Marching single-file down the driveway came what looked for all the world like a dozen large, pointy-ended, overturned orange bugs, each propelled by a pair of human legs. Leading the procession was a longer-legged bug, and all the bugs were singing lustily.

Jace laughed at her astonishment. "Inflatable kayaks," he explained. "Each boy has to take one to the river, and putting it on top your head is the easiest way to carry it. That's Mac, our chaplain and history teacher, coming along in front. You remember him?"

Katy didn't remember the long-legged African American, of course, and she was too slow in concealing her blank response for Jace not to notice.

"He conducted the memorial service for your parents in our chapel."

"Yes, of course," she murmured, still watching the strange procession. Several moments later she was surprised to realize

Jace was still standing beside her, an odd expression on his face. Reflective? Puzzled?

"You're not wearing much makeup these days."

The unexpected personal comment, with a faint undertone of approval, startled her. Had she always gone in for heavy makeup before? She'd unpacked a cosmopolitan variety of cosmetics scattered among the cartons shipped from New York, but it hadn't occurred to her to apply more than sunscreen and a touch of lipstick for an outing such as this.

"No, perhaps not." Then, feeling flustered by his continuing appraisal and nearness, she added lightly, "But I am hiding under this big hat."

"I guess I'm surprised you're not hiding in the—" He broke off as if suddenly embarrassed she might interpret this as his thinking she *should* hide somewhere.

"I just meant you've never been one to—" Again he floundered and broke off. He lifted the cap a fraction of an inch, as if it were suddenly in urgent need of adjustment, and smoothed his hair.

"Never been one to tarnish my model image by doing something such as appearing in public almost bald?" she filled in lightly.

"Something like that," he admitted. He smiled, and his eyes were a tantalizing blend of brown and green-gold flecks, and good humor. "I like it." He tilted her floppy-brimmed hat at a more rakish angle, and for a moment Katy's breath caught as she thought his fingertips were going to brush her face. But all he did was close the door lightly.

Jace detoured the marching procession and followed an overgrown lane through the woods, stopping once to take a chain saw out of the back of the pickup and efficiently buzz through a couple of fallen trees blocking the way. He'd apparently anticipated a need for repair work after the old dirt road hadn't been used for months.

Katy breathed deeply of the earthy scent of the thick forest around them, everything so vibrantly alive and green and growing, as if, should the pickup pause too long, some eager vine might twine around it. Branches brushed her elbow hanging out the window, and off to one side neon pink ribbons fluttered on the survey stakes Mrs. L. had mentioned. Once a trio of deer bounded down the lane ahead of them, the height of their leaps belying the slender fragility of their legs. Oh, how Katy wished she didn't have the cast tying her down, that she, too, could run and leap! Did she really plan to sell this wonderful piece of heaven-on-earth and dash off to the tinsel glitz of Hollywood?

"Would you like to get out?" Jace asked when they reached the river. "There's a log by the fire pit where you can sit."

The narrow strip of main current ran fast and wild on the far side of the river, white water spraying around exposed rocks, but on this side the water lapped on a wide, shallow, half-moon of sandy beach. The calm, almost lakelike stretch of green water didn't actually feel threatening to Katy, but it did make her want to keep her distance. "I think I'll just watch from here, thanks."

"I'll get a fire started, then. We always get soaked on these excursions and need to dry off and warm up." He started away from the pickup, then paused and looked back. They'd both been cordial so far, even cautiously friendly for a few moments, but now a hint of hostility resurfaced. "Although our agreement didn't cover building fires."

"Just do what you've always done."

She watched as he gathered twigs and larger pieces of wood, moving with the easy grace of an athlete and starting the fire with the competence of an experienced woodsman. The flames crackled briskly by the time the procession of boys and kayaks arrived. Katy couldn't dredge up any happy memories of campfires, yet she found the scene inviting. If it weren't that she'd have to ask for Jace's help to get out of the pickup, she'd have gone to sit by the fire.

First came the donning of life jackets; Jace's cardinal rule was that no one got near the water without one, instructors included. He unloaded his own kayak from the pickup, paddled out about fifteen feet, and from there coached the boys on shore in proper use and handling of their equipment. When they were allowed to try it on their own, he stood waist deep in the water with them, moving from boy to boy to correct the holding of a paddle or balance of weight or show how to dig deep to make a turn. Mac, in his own kayak, took up a farther-out position, guarding against any accidental or intentional run toward the dangerous rough water. Boys being boys, a couple of the more rambunctious quickly dumped themselves in the water, but Jace maintained a nice balance between lessons in technique and safety and letting them have fun. Within minutes, the boys were scooting around like so many noisy orange water bugs, and Jace waded out to warm and dry himself at the fire.

From the shadowed interior of the pickup Katy watched him curiously. He had so much patience with the boys, and they obviously respected and liked him. If she could only come right out and ask him about what had happened between herself and him. Then she had to laugh because, absorbed in watching the boys, he let his steaming backside get too close to the fire and jumped away with a yelp.

She didn't think he could have heard her laugh, but suddenly he turned and stalked toward the pickup. Without a word he yanked the door open and scooted her into his arms.

70

"What are you *doing?*" she yelped.

"I decided you'd like to sit by the fire but were just too stubborn to ask for my help."

That observation was so accurate that Katy couldn't even think of an appropriate put-down for the high-handed, macho way he carried her to the fire. He deposited her on the log and asked if she'd like something to drink. "There's Pepsi and 7UP in the pickup."

"No, thank you."

"Looks as if I got you a little damp. Sorry about that."

She was indeed a "little damp" along one side, soaked actually, from being clamped against his wet clothes, but it was difficult to maintain an aloof air of injury when she was so pleased to be sitting there by the crackling flames, wrapped in the fragrance of woodsmoke and feeling the pleasantly rough bark of the log beneath her. "I'm fine."

He carefully selected a long stick from the pile by the fire and solemnly handed it to her. "I can't sit beside a campfire without wanting to poke at it."

Katy couldn't either, she realized, and delightedly she jabbed and watched the sparks spiral upward. Yet she also couldn't help clinging to a huffy attitude for the way he'd high-handedly hauled her over here like a sack of cement.

"Isn't this a school day?" she asked in a deliberately challenging tone. "How come your students are out here rather than in a classroom?"

"The boys who come to Damascus are mostly urban, from troubled families and usually in trouble themselves. Their closest contact with nature has probably been loitering on a street corner. We aren't the type of school that specializes in teaching rigorous outdoor survival techniques, but we try to teach the boys something about various types of *life* survival, from the physical to the intellectual, with the foundation of a spiritual connection with God. We want them to learn the basics of work and play and worship, how to be both team players and independent thinkers so they can resist the wrong kind of peer pressure back home. And not all that can be learned in a classroom."

Jace started out simply explaining, but a fierce passion rose in his voice as he spoke, an urgent sense of purpose and strength of dedication coming through that deeply impressed Katy.

"These twelve boys are all the students you have?"

"No. We average about forty, all in the sixth, seventh, and eighth grades, but we usually take no more than twelve or fifteen boys on outings such as this. We hope to expand the school to include older boys later, but expansion takes money, of course. And we need to upgrade the facilities for some of our current classes, especially in the area of computers. I'm hoping for a corporate donation to buy new equipment in the near future."

"Did you come from a Christian home? Or were you also a boy in trouble from a troubled family?" Katy asked impulsively.

He gave her an odd look, and it occurred to her they may have had this conversation sometime in the past. A sudden splashing from the water made him look in that direction, where at least half the boys were now involved in a spirited waterfight.

"Okay, you guys, knock off the horseplay," he called. "We're going to run some races in a few minutes." His tone was good-natured but authoritative, and the boys "knocked it off." He turned his attention back to Katy, but instead of backing her into a corner about her faulty memory as she'd expected, he said skeptically, "You were never interested in my background or family before."

She wasn't? How odd. "I am now." When he didn't immediately offer any information, she approached from a different angle. "Jace. That's an unusual name."

"My father was something of a gambler and wanted to name me Ace. My mother wanted Jock. So perhaps I'm fortunate they agreed on nothing worse than Jace." He smiled wryly. "It was probably the only thing they ever agreed on."

"So it wasn't exactly a Brady Bunch childhood."

He shrugged lightly. "I was never into gangs or drugs, but I was always a troublemaker. I had a chip on my shoulder and a temper to go with it. My mother abandoned us before I started school. My dad was a good mechanic, but he was also a drinker and brawler, so we bounced around a lot. I remember going to four different schools one year."

"That couldn't have been easy," Katy said sympathetically, catching a glimpse of an always-the-outsider boy behind this confident man.

He shrugged again, this time in dismissal of what had to have been a bumpy childhood and adolescence. "But I managed to get a football scholarship to college and went professional when I graduated. I bounced around some there, too, and eventually got my right knee pretty well messed up."

"So then you decided to quit football and start the school?"

He shook his head emphatically. "No. I wasn't a Christian then. And leaving football wasn't what I wanted. But between my injured knee and my ongoing temper problems, I hadn't much choice. For a while I tried to get into sportscasting or coaching." He smiled a little grimly. "But I wasn't exactly deluged with offers. I was bitter and angry and resentful and envious, and I started going downhill, fast."

He didn't offer details, but Katy could guess, especially with the role model he had in his father.

"But a friend...well, not really a friend," he amended, "at least not at the time, because I steered away from 'religious' guys, but a Christian guy I'd played ball with, saw what was happening. He literally hauled me off to backpack in the mountains in Montana. It was more isolated and wild than anything I'd ever seen, barely a deer path in the wilderness, and I was mad, really furious with him for dragging me out there. For the first two days all that kept me from stomping out was a head-pounding hangover, plus the fact that I was pretty well lost. But then I sobered up and started to enjoy it, and finally something happened to me. We were sitting under the stars one night, and Cork was just kind of musing about how many stars God had made and was he still making new ones, and wasn't it something fantastic that God cared for each one of us, insignificant as we were in the midst of all this, that he loved us so much his own Son came to us. And suddenly, as if a light snapped on in my head, all the stuff Cork had been trying to get through to me became *real*. It wasn't just meaningless words anymore. It all made sense, and I sat there just feeling *enveloped* in the Lord's love."

Jace broke off as the memory of the awe and wonder of those moments obviously came back to him, and Katy felt within herself an odd stirring of yearning for…what? She didn't know, but suddenly a small light came on in her own head.

"And that's why, when you started the school, you named it Damascus! Because on a mountain trail in Montana you had this life-changing experience like Paul's, when he met the Lord on the road to Damascus!"

"A bit presumptuous of me, because my experience couldn't come close to Paul's, but I would like to help the boys find the glorious immersion in his love that came to me that night—" He broke off again, a surprised look on his face. "What do you know about Paul and his road-to-Damascus experience? As I recall, you always had more faith in the Easter

74

bunny than in Jesus, and what you knew about the Bible would fit on the end of a mascara brush," he added bluntly.

"I don't know," she said slowly, as puzzled as she had been earlier when her knowledge about Samson and his shorn hair had popped up. Why and how did she know these things?

"Did something happen to you in the last few months, Kat...Katy? Some spiritual awakening of your own that made you read the Bible?"

She remembered her rejection of Dr. Fischer's Pastor Ross, and now that same hostile feeling surged forward again. *No entrance here!* She was not going to sit here and be questioned and preached to by Jace as if she were one of his wayward boys.

"No," she snapped curtly. She may have acquired some unexplained biblical knowledge, but she had not metamorphosed into a devout believer. "I'd rather not talk about this anymore," she added stiffly.

If Jace intended to pursue this subject in spite of her objections, he didn't have a chance. A herd of shivering, noisy boys descended on the campfire, spraying water like wet puppies and good-naturedly jostling for space closest to the heat. After the boys warmed up, Jace presided over races, varying the competition from speed to accuracy to expertise at turns to give each boy a chance to show off individual skills. The outing ended with a football-type huddle for a brief prayer, and then, to Katy's surprise, the boys trooped over to give her awkward but sincere thanks for letting them come here to enjoy the river.

After the "orange bug" procession started back toward the school, Jace carried water from the river to douse the fire and checked to make sure no equipment had been left behind. Katy's crutches were still in the pickup, so all she could do was sit and wait. She stiffened when he picked her up, carefully not letting a single inch more of her body touch his than was absolutely unavoidable. She did not let one arm go around his neck as she now realized had happened before, and she did not acknowledge the appeal of his muscular strength and the damp warmth and smoky scent that clung to him.

The door frame knocked her hat askew as he scooted her into the pickup. She plopped it back on her head.

"Are you afraid of a spiritual experience, Katy?" he asked gently, his arms still between her and the seat.

She squirmed away. "I don't believe in spiritual experiences!"

"You didn't sound like it when you compared my experience to Paul's on the road to Damascus."

"If there is a God, I don't think he gives a hoot about most of us. Or maybe he just abandons or forgets us **if** we don't live up to his standards or he's in a bad mood or something."

Jace tilted his head. "Are you referring to something in particular, Katy?"

"Not necessarily," she had to admit. But even if she couldn't remember what was behind her hostility, she could feel it welling up in an icy fountain from her heart.

"The Lord forgives when we ask him to, Katy. He doesn't condemn. And even if we abandon him, he never forgets or abandons us. He doesn't give up on us even if we give up on him. He's working in our lives whether or not we recognize it at the time. 'God is our refuge and strength, an ever-present help in trouble.'"

She recognized his last words as a quote from somewhere in Psalms, but she refused to acknowledge that. All she said was a stiff, "I'll think about that."

He nodded slowly. "Yes, I think you will." He smoothed a wisp of hair valiantly trying to grow above her ear. "Katy, no matter how you try to deny it, you *are* different now. You've changed during these past months. You'd never even have considered 'thinking about it' before." He smiled. "And I rather like the new and improved Kat 'Katy' Cavanaugh."

She didn't want to feel warmed by that comment, but she couldn't help a faint glow that started where his fingertip lightly caressed a point behind her ear.

"Would you like to come to services in our chapel this Sunday? And maybe stay for dinner afterward? We eat cafeteria style during the week, but Sunday is a sit-down dinner."

She hesitated, oddly drawn by the invitation. But then another light came on in her mind, and she jerked away from the tempting touch of his fingertips. "No, thank you." To herself she added, *And if you think you can get me to go through with the land donation by buttering me up, think again!*

They drove back to the house in silence.

Seven

The more she thought about it, the stronger Katy felt that Jace had simply been trying to butter her up in hopes of getting the land donation revived. Complimenting her, carrying her as if she were some featherweight princess, offering friendly invitations. She didn't know why this realization of the motive behind his actions should hurt as well as make her angry, but it did.

She saw several cars drive under the swinging sign at the school's entrance on Sunday morning, which pointed out to her that what she'd received wasn't some exclusive invitation. Anyone in the surrounding area who wanted to come to the services was obviously welcome. She was standing by the window, feeling restless, when the sound of an old-fashioned church bell startled her. It rang out from across the road, pealing across forest and meadow and hills with a serene but joyous majesty, gloriously pure and beautiful, and it called to something deep inside her.

She stood at the open window of the bedroom, her breathing shallow, fists clenched around her crutches, as the sound rolled through her like a melodic heartbeat. Mt. Shasta glistened in the sun as if frosted with celestial crystals, an iridescent hummingbird momentarily hovered in her face, and a scent almost unbearably fresh and sweet drifted up from the green meadow. God's creations. Again an unknown yearning tugged at her like a powerful tide swirling around and through her.

And then came a strange, aching loneliness as the sound of

the bell faded away and only an echoing silence remained.

A pan clattered in the kitchen, and she abruptly snapped out of the odd spell. Of course there was loneliness, but it had nothing to do with a noisy bell shattering the peace of an otherwise gorgeous morning. She'd lost her parents and her past, and her future hung like a question mark before her; she'd be abnormal if she *didn't* feel lonely.

She brushed away a tear that had started down her cheek and determinedly clomped off to the kitchen. She'd had an urge to try her hand at cooking the last couple of days, and this was as good a time as any to do it. Mrs. L. appeared astonished by her sudden desire to make a pie but quickly cooperated by bringing out a cookbook and helping her locate flour and shortening and suggesting peaches from the freezer as a filling.

"Haven't I always liked to cook?" Katy asked. She couldn't *remember* making pies, but cutting the shortening into the flour felt pleasingly familiar. She had to brace herself against the counter as she worked, but it felt wonderful to be doing something.

"You loved to putter in the kitchen with me when you were little, but I don't think you did much cooking in New York. I had the impression you ate out most of the time. Or dieted."

Mrs. L. thawed the frozen peaches in the microwave. She watched with a delighted smile as Katy rolled out the dough and neatly fluted the edges of the top crust over the filling. And when the fragrant, flaky pie came out of the oven, she declared it as good or better than any she'd ever done herself.

"Oh, Katy, it's so wonderful to have you back, so much more like you were when you were a little girl." Mrs. L. hugged her impulsively, and they both laughed as button-tailed, jealous Tillie tried to sharpen her claws on Katy's cast.

Making the pie took care of the morning, but Katy still felt restless as she wandered from window to window. Mrs. L.

asked if she'd like to look at photographs again, but she was tired of the frustration of trying to breathe life into a dead past. It would be a wonderful afternoon for hiking. Which she couldn't do, of course. Or swimming. She shuddered lightly. No, even if she weren't weighed down with the cast, not swimming. Just watching the rough water on the far side of the river had made her feel uneasy. But they could take a spin in the red-toy convertible!

She enthusiastically enlarged on the idea as she presented it to Mrs. L. "We can pack a lunch and have a little picnic!"

"Oh, I don't think so, sweetie," Mrs. L. said doubtfully. "The convertible has a stick shift, and I haven't driven a stick shift in years."

"So you kill the engine or get it in the wrong gear or something. Who cares?" Katy said gaily. "C'mon, let's do it!"

"But it hasn't been driven since you were here last. It might not even start."

"We won't know unless we try, will we? Let's pack a lunch and give it a try."

Mrs. L. still seemed doubtful, but she put together a salad while Katy made ham-and-cheese sandwiches. Seeing Katy piling fat slices of onion on one sandwich, Mrs. L. finally seemed to catch her enthusiasm and laughed.

"Better put some on my sandwich, too. With you breathing onion fire, I think I'm going to need some in self-defense."

By the time Mrs. L. backed the convertible out of the garage in a series of jerky hops, they were both giggling. A jolt forward and a quick engine death when Mrs. L. got in the wrong gear brought more giggles.

"Which way?" Mrs. L. asked when she finally braked cautiously at the main road.

"I've already been that way," Katy said, motioning toward Wilding. "Let's be adventurous and try the other direction."

This time Mrs. L. got into the right gear, but she pressed too hard on the accelerator, and they took off as if they were in the Indy 500, squirting gravel like rocky lightning.

"Whee!" Katy said.

"Whoa!" Mrs. L. corrected, pulling the eager convertible down to a more sedate pace.

"Gas?" Katy asked suddenly.

"You check. I don't dare take my eyes off the road. I think this little rascal would take off and fly if I'd let it!"

Katy leaned over and checked various dials on the dashboard. The gas gauge showed almost full. "We can make it to the moon and back," she declared confidently.

They met no cars on the road, and even log trucks weren't running on a Sunday, but once, to Katy's astonishment a bear and two cubs dashed across the road in front of them. She felt gloriously carefree in the open convertible, at one with mountains and sky and sunshine. A balmy current of pine-scented air flowed against her skin and teased the scarf anchoring her hat. Sunlight shafting between the trunks of tall firs and pine created a dazzling light-and-shadows show as they slipped into a living tunnel created by an overhead canopy of branches. A herd of deer grazed among blue wildflowers along a meandering stream in a meadow, the scent of tall grass damp and lush. The engine purred like a lazy cat, with a reassuring growl of power on the steep hills.

They finally stopped at a tiny forest service campground with just three picnic tables, a half dozen resident squirrels, and a soft matting of old pine needles underfoot. The bright-eyed squirrels wouldn't come close, but a bold bluejay hopped to within a few feet of the table to pick up bits of bread crust Katy tossed him. In the open air the sandwiches and salad and pie tasted fantastic, the lemonade from a Thermos better than lush champagne. Mrs. L. had brought a camera along, and they snapped clowning-around pictures of each other and the squirrels and bluejay.

After the late lunch Mrs. L. brought out pen and paper and settled down to write a long letter to Evan, and Katy leaned against the curve of an oak tree and dozed peacefully. Later they finished up the leftovers and lingered until the cooling air and lengthening shadows made Katy reluctantly say they'd better start home.

Then a small problem surfaced. A control button plainly indicated that it should raise the top of the convertible, but all the button did when pressed was growl ominously. After giving up on the uncooperative button, they spent an even longer time trying to figure out if the top could be raised manually.

The last rays of sunlight had already left the forested hilltops to the east, and the road was in blue-shadowed dusk by the time they decided to settle for a chilly, open-air ride home. Katy was relieved that there were no problems with the headlights when Mrs. L. flicked that switch, and the gas gauge still showed a comforting half full.

But Mrs. L. fussed as she glanced across the low bucket seats at Katy. "Oh dear, this worries me. You mustn't catch cold, not along with everything else."

The air blowing into the open vehicle was no longer the balmy caress it had been in the afternoon sunshine, but Katy quickly said, "I'm fine," even as the cold raised goosebumps on her skin. She wrapped her arms around herself and tried to burrow into the seat.

Out of nowhere, like an entity materializing out of thin air, a dark figure leaped into the headlights. Two eyes glowed in the beams, frozen as if paralyzed by the light. "Watch out!" Katy screamed. She grabbed the door frame. "We're going to hit it—"

Mrs. L. slammed the brakes so hard they squealed. She

twisted the steering wheel, and the tires skidded sideways on gravel. The flag of dust following the car enveloped them in a choking cloud. But in relief Katy saw the frightened deer bound safely across the road and vanish into a seemingly impenetrable wall of forest. She sagged against the leather seat and briefly closed her eyes, shaken but relieved they hadn't injured or killed the innocent animal.

The jolting stop had killed the engine. It also must have thrown the headlights out of kilter, Katy thought, because they now pointed crazily skyward, illuminating the tops of the dark trees. Then she realized the whole car was tilted at a disoriented angle. She peered over the side and saw the bottom of the ditch barely inches below her.

"We slid off the road," Mrs. L. announced shakily. Still clutching the steering wheel, she peered down at Katy from her higher position in the tilted car. "Are you okay?"

"I think so. Good thing we were wearing our seat belts."

"Just let me sit here a minute and stop shaking, and then I'll see if the engine will start again."

Finally, after wiping her hands nervously on her pants, Mrs. L. tried the engine. It started nicely, and they looked at each other in relief. But when she shifted into first and eased her foot down on the gas, the engine simply growled uselessly as the tires dug ever deeper into the slope of the ditch. The car slid farther sideways, so steeply angled now that Katy was almost lying against the door.

"Oh, no, we can't be stuck out here!" Even with the car tilted at the awkward angle, Mrs. L. frantically jammed the accelerator to the floor. The useless straining of the engine rose to a squeal, and Katy covered her head as the spinning wheels sprayed dirt and weeds and gravel.

A hot scent of oil, grease, and rubber boiled up around them, and Katy came out from under the sheltering cover of her arms to put a restraining hand on Mrs. L.'s arm. "Maybe we'd better let it cool down."

Mrs. L. didn't have to turn the engine off. It suddenly gave a strangled gasp and died, and silence settled around them with the soft flutter of falling dust.

"I wonder how far we are from home?" Katy tried to keep a small panic out of her voice.

"*Miles.* Oh, Katy, what are we going to do?" Mrs. L. sounded on the brink of a much larger panic.

Katy loosened the scarf and shook the dust out of her hat. What *were* they going to do? There were not apt to be any helpful passersby. No one lived out this way. It was all government-owned forest land beyond her place and Damascus. She obviously couldn't try to walk anywhere. With the convertible angled into the ditch she doubted she could even get the door open, much less crawl out it.

At this point Jace would no doubt advise prayer. That was what people did in times of crisis, wasn't it? But she'd prayed before, and—

Deep in her mind, something glimmered just beyond the edge of identification. She'd prayed before and...*what*? She strained at the dark glimpse of something, struggling as if with a door that had cracked open but would go no farther. Had she prayed when she was injured and abandoned on the beach?

She swallowed and abruptly abandoned this line of thought.

She glanced across at Mrs. L. who was still gripping the steering wheel as if it were the rail of a sinking ship. Could Mrs. L. walk out for help? Katy doubted it, and, in all honesty, she had no desire to be trapped alone in the open car in the dark. She tried to keep her voice confident as she came up with the only possible solution.

"There'll be log trucks going by in the morning. We'll just

have to wait until one comes by to help us." She determinedly ignored how many long, chilly hours separated now from then. "It's going to be cold and uncomfortable sitting here all night, but I'm sure we're in no real danger."

"A couple of years ago a hunter was badly mauled by a bear up here somewhere." Mrs. L.'s voice was small and scared. "And one with cubs is the most dangerous kind." She didn't have to remind Katy about the mother bear and cubs they'd seen.

"But we aren't out here doing something to annoy the wildlife." Katy tried to sound amused rather than frightened by Mrs. L.'s dire bear story. She had the feeling that Mrs. L. might give in to hysterics if Katy let her own fear show.

"Neither was he. He was just in his tent, sleeping. And I've heard that sometimes there are hidden marijuana patches way out here in the mountains, and the people who grow them don't take kindly to strangers poking around."

"I don't think we're going to be mistaken for marijuana-patch pirates or drug agents," Katy said lightly. "We look like just what we are, two women in a car that slid off the road."

Two vulnerable, helpless women in an expensive, open convertible that might be worth stealing even in its present awkward condition. Murder had been committed for less.

A veil of silence settled around them again. Except that now small, furtive sounds filtered through the veil. Gurgles and hisses of the cooling engine. Unidentified rustles in the dark wall of forest beyond the ditch. A strange bird call. A bat swooped down from above, and Mrs. L. shrieked and waved her arms wildly around her ducked head.

"Please, Mrs. L., we have to remain calm—"

Which was not going to be easy, Katy realized grimly, as light flared around the bend in the road, and two headlights bore down on them out of the darkness. Then her hopes rose.

Jace? Jace roaring up like a knight who'd traded his white horse for a four-wheel-drive pickup?

No. A van, pulling up close, then backing away and angling to target the blinding blaze of headlights directly in their eyes. Behind the glare the large, dark shadow of a man stepped down from the driver's seat. And two more shadowy figures climbed out the opposite door.

Eight

"Lenore?"

"Joe? Is that you, Joe?" Mrs. L. called eagerly.

Katy shaded her eyes against the blinding glare. One of the dark silhouettes knelt to peer under the car. Mac, she realized, as the light caught his face. And then a voice spoke almost over her head.

"Are you hurt?"

She twisted in the seat to peer up at Jace looming over her side of the tilted car. Relief and gratitude that he was here washed over her, yet her next thought was resentment that here she was in another predicament needing his help.

"I think I'm okay. But I can't get out—"

"We'll get you out." Jace's voice gritted rough and angry even as he offered reassurance. "But didn't it occur to you that in your condition you shouldn't be out chasing around in the mountains after dark?"

"We didn't plan to be out after dark! But a deer jumped in front of the car."

He cut off her explanation. "We'll discuss this later."

By this time Joe had helped Mrs. L. climb out of the car and was now tucking a coat around her shoulders. With rather less gallantry, Jace tossed a coat to Katy and let her struggle into it herself.

The three men held a conference in the headlights. Then Joe went around to the rear of the van and returned with a chain. Jace scooted into the ditch and fastened the chain to something under the car. Mac turned the van around, backed up to the convertible and Jace slid in beside Katy. A few moments later, pulled by the van, the convertible lunged up out of the ditch like a bucking bronc. Jace braked it to a smooth stop inches from the van.

As promised, he had gotten her out of the predicament.

He rode in the open convertible on the way home because someone had to be at the steering wheel while the car was towed. Mac drove the van, Mrs. L. snuggled up against Joe, and Katy huddled under the coat.

At the house, the engine still wouldn't start, so the three men pushed the small convertible into the garage. Joe said he'd take a look at it in a day or two. Katy offered pie and coffee if the men wanted to come in and warm up. Jace looked half frozen, and Katy guiltily realized it was his coat she'd been wearing on the drive home. Mac declined the offer for coffee, saying he needed to talk to one of the boys before bedtime. He jogged back to the school on foot, but Joe and Jace followed the women inside. Mrs. L. served the pie and coffee and then disappeared to take a hot bath.

"You take the van and go on home," Jace said casually to Joe after they finished the pie. "I'll be along in a few minutes."

Joe left by the back door. Jace looked at Katy. She wrapped her hands around the coffee mug.

"We went on a little afternoon picnic," she said defensively. Then, because she couldn't help being curious, she added, "How did you happen to come out there?"

"When I didn't see lights on here after dark I came over to check and found the garage door open. I went back and asked if anyone had seen the convertible leave, and a couple of the boys said it had headed toward the mountains. I figured we'd better run out and take a look."

"We appreciate that." Katy did appreciate the concern, but the fact that she had to acknowledge that he'd again dashed to her rescue kept a certain stiffness in her voice. "Thank you."

She braced herself for criticism, but instead Jace asked, "You really made that pie?"

"Yes."

Joe had earlier praised the pie as if it were some blue-ribbon accomplishment, but if she expected glowing praise from Jace, she was mistaken. He simply studied her across the breakfast nook for so long that she drew fidgety little circles with the coffee cup on the table. She was still wearing the ribboned hat, but it felt like scant protection against his appraisal, as if he could see right through to skimpy blond tufts and scars and layers of road dust, perhaps even smell onion breath. But when he spoke she realized that it was not physical shortcomings he was assessing.

"Another change," he said with a reflective tilt of head. "First you turn up with this new Bible knowledge. You change your mind about the boys using the river. You tone down the makeup. And now you come up with this sudden inclination toward pie-making domesticity."

Katy glanced up sharply at the odd listing. On the surface it sounded grudgingly complimentary, yet *skepticism* ran like a dark undercurrent beneath the words. She didn't understand. Why should he be skeptical, almost as if he suspected she were faking the very qualities he seemed to admire? She wasn't faking anything. If she was different now, it was genuine change caused by what had happened to her. Almost angrily she snapped, "Dr. Fischer said there might be personality changes after—"

She broke off, instantly realizing from his sudden alertness that she'd carelessly leaped in the wrong direction. "After my accident," she finished lamely. She glanced at the owl-shaped clock on the kitchen wall. "Look, I'm really tired and dirty, and—"

Jace didn't let her off with that plea. He instantly pounced on the imprecise statement about an accident. "Why would a doctor think an accident might cause personality changes?" When she didn't respond, he leaned forward, forearms on the table, and relentlessly dug deeper. "Are you talking about a surgical doctor or a psychiatrist?"

"What difference does it make?" she flared. "There's nothing wrong with seeing a psychiatrist."

"Of course not. I just want to understand. Have you had special treatments of some kind, Katy? Electroshock, perhaps, or drugs?"

"No! I just broke my leg and had scalp injuries that needed stitches."

"And changed," he stated flatly. Then he leaned back and gave her another appraisal, this time with a hard ruthlessness in those hazel eyes. "Unless this is all some elaborate put-on, of course."

"Put-on?" she repeated, a feeling of bafflement now overlaying her agitation.

"Maybe this is all some complicated little game you're playing to amuse yourself while your leg heals. Or perhaps you decided to get in a bit of real-life acting practice before you storm Hollywood? So you give yourself a *real* acting challenge, turning the old spiteful Kat into sweet, virtuous, domestic Katy. And that's quite a stretch, isn't it?"

The sarcasm was so harsh and the accusation so startling that Katy gasped. Suddenly she remembered back to when she'd first called him for help when she was trapped under the chest in the bedroom, and how he'd suspiciously asked if the call was "some kind of trick." That had puzzled her then, and it still did. And being virtuous and domestic was *acting?*

"Oh, come on, don't look so shocked and innocent. Ever

since you came back you've acted as if that night never happened."

"What night?" Katy asked in dismay.

"Now you're going to pretend you don't even remember it? C'mon, Kat," he scoffed. "You call me up with some song and dance about a prowler trying to get in the house, and when I get over here there's no prowler, just you in a sheer black nightie, scented candles in the bedroom, two glasses of wine. Oh, that's good, Kat, very good, very realistic with the appalled, horrified look, as if you don't remember."

"I don't!" Katy cried. "I don't remember anything about this. I don't remember anything about you or my folks or this house or my *life!*"

They stared at each other over the now cold coffee.

His eyes narrowed. "I don't get it. What do you mean?"

She lifted her chin and stared at him defiantly. Okay, she'd revealed her secret, which she hadn't intended to do. But it was out now, and she didn't really care. "I mean the time before I woke up in a hospital in Oregon is a blank. I have…not exactly memories, but *knowledge* about a lot of the everyday things of life. I can read and write and do math. I know *trivia.* What the relationship is between characters on TV shows. That Alan Jackson and Garth Brooks are popular country-and-western singers. That the Space Needle is in Seattle and California has earthquakes. But until Mrs. L. saw my photo in a newspaper and showed up to identify me, I didn't know a thing about *me.* And I can't even *imagine* myself doing what you say I did!"

"Amnesia?" he said slowly, doubtfully, as if he were examining the word like a flawed piece of machinery. "I've heard of it, everybody has. But I'm not sure I've ever believed it actually happens in real life."

"Believe it," Katy muttered.

"And the doctor said personality changes sometimes occur with amnesia?"

Katy nodded. "I'd appreciate it if you wouldn't tell anyone else about this. Mrs. L. and I discussed it and agreed that people are often judgmental and unkind about mental problems. I think she's more concerned than I am, but there's really no need for anyone to know. The doctor said that in time I should recover." She hesitated and then had to add truthfully, "Probably."

"But not necessarily?"

"Not necessarily."

"This was all caused by an accident?"

She sketched the details of what she knew about being found injured on the beach without identification. "I have no idea how I got there. About three months earlier, perhaps shortly after the…bedroom scene you mentioned, I'd told Mrs. L. I wanted to get away and think for a while, and she took me into Redding to meet a friend or friends. I never contacted her after that; although, since I told her to have my roommates ship all my belongings out here, I must not have intended to return to New York."

"And you have no idea where you were or what you were doing during those three months?" He sounded more per-plexed than skeptical now.

"I have no memory of where I was or what I was doing dur-ing my *entire life.*"

He covered her hand with his, his face troubled. "Katy, I'm sorry."

Whether he was offering sympathy for her problems or an apology for his rough words, she was uncertain. She pulled her hand away. "Apparently you can fill me in on some of my activi-ties. Exactly what was our relationship before this night I called you about a prowler?"

"Katy, I don't think we need to go into any of this now."

"Yes," she said quietly, "I think we do."

He got up and added fresh coffee to both their cups as if stalling for time.

She smiled wryly. "You don't need to gloss it over. I want to know exactly the kind of person I really am. How long have we known each other?"

"We met when your folks invited me over for dinner one time two or three years ago when you were here visiting. You were very charming. A little flirty. But I didn't see it as any special interest in me. It was just the way you were: see a reasonably attractive male and you automatically went into make-a-conquest mode."

"And did I make a conquest?"

"I saw you as beautiful and vivacious and charming. You could make a man feel as if he was the only person in the room." He paused reflectively. "The only person in the *universe*. You were also as shallow as a lipstick smear."

She'd asked for honesty. She was getting it.

"But you were pretty broken up when your parents were killed. I was the one who called you right after the plane crash. And while you were here and seemed so lost and bewildered, we talked about my Christian faith and how it related to death."

"And?"

"You listened, but afterwards you just shrugged it all off. You said that you thought this life was all we had, that you intended to grab all you could in it, and I was a fool for throwing my life away on a bunch of delinquents out here in the sticks."

"Oh, Jace," Katy murmured, appalled. She still felt a surge of hostility at the thought of any personal relationship with God for herself, obviously a holdover from the old Kat, but she certainly couldn't deny the value of what he was doing with the boys.

"You weren't really antagonistic toward the Lord. You simply dismissed everything I said as a pleasant myth, something like the tooth fairy and Santa Claus. You didn't stay long then, but by the time you came back three or four months ago, the estate was settled and you were ready to sell the ranch."

"And I went back on my parents' plan to donate half of it to Damascus."

He frowned slightly. "You remember that?"

"No, I don't. Mrs. L. told me. She's been giving me a crash course in .my past. Kat Cavanaugh 101, you might call it. Although, so far, I'm afraid I'm flunking. Anyway, when you then wanted to buy the land, I turned you down."

"Not only turned me down, you laughed at the offer. Although I must say you laughed at it quite charmingly. You teased that I ought to let you talk to some of our sponsors, that you'd bet *you* could lure some very generous donations out of them."

Katy felt color flow into her face at the self-centered confidence in her own flirty powers implied by those words. "You and I were still on friendly terms at that time?"

"More or less. You had me over for dinner a couple of times, and once you went horseback riding with me and the boys. Another time you came over for a wiener roast. But you were pretty piqued because I didn't give you the kind of attention you usually received from men. Eventually, after I turned down several of your suggestions, including spending a skiing weekend together, I think you began to look on me as a challenge."

"Challenge?"

"You were obviously accustomed to winding any man you wanted around your little finger. When I didn't 'wind' properly, you turned up the heat. You made it plain you were interested in a relationship of a more intimate nature."

The faint color in Katy's cheeks blazed to a full embarrassed blush now. "I tried to get you to marry me?"

He laughed without humor. "Marriage? Oh, no. Marrying a guy running a Christian school in the sticks was definitely not one of your goals in life. But you apparently found me attractive enough for a temporary fling while you were here. So you set up the prowler scene with the idea that not even straight-laced Jace Foster could resist that on-the-spot bedroom opportunity when it was offered. When I *did* resist, you turned furious. You hurled a glass of wine at me, screamed that I was something less than a man, and told me to get out. The next day you called up and announced that if I or anyone else from Damascus ever came on this place again, you'd call the sheriff and have us charged with trespassing."

Katy didn't know what to say. She didn't want to believe what he said, but she couldn't doubt it. There was also proof in that wine-dark stain she saw every day on the bedroom carpet. She could understand now why he'd been so astonished, even angry, when she called for help, and she understood, too, why he wanted her change of mind about crossing the property in writing.

She swallowed and finally murmured, "You've been very kind, after all that." She lifted her gaze and tried to smile. "The good Christian attitude, turn the other cheek?"

"I believe in that Christian philosophy, although I sometimes have a struggle with it in practice," he admitted. "I really had to grit my teeth to come over here the day you called me. But since then...You *are* different now, Katy."

He reached across the table and with a fingertip tilted her chin so their eyes met. "I was so worried when I realized you were still out there in the mountains."

"*You*, worried about *me?*" She tried to smile and keep her voice light, but both smile and voice wobbled.

"Yes."

Slowly and deliberately he leaned across the open space between them and kissed her. Katy had no specific memory of kisses, but secondhand knowledge of her past told her she'd been kissed, and the feeling was not totally unfamiliar. Yet at the same time there was a sparkling, first-kiss newness to the feel of his lips on hers, a heady blend of honey and spice, sensitivity and ardency. Or was it that she'd simply never known a kiss like this? The caring and sweet tenderness and gentle passion of this kiss curled around her heart. A physical glow drifted through her body, and an emotional warmth infiltrated her mind and the vulnerable emptiness of her heart. For the first time within her short memory she felt secure, as if she were where she belonged. A little shyly, she returned the kiss, her hand creeping up to wrap around the back of his neck.

But, even with the protective shield of his lips still on hers, a sudden doubt slithered through her. Had she really changed, deep down and permanently? Or was it only a "lipstick smear" of a change, surface deep, destined to vanish when her memory returned?

"Jace," she asked huskily when he finally lifted his head, "have you ever kissed me before?"

"No."

"I'm glad you did now."

"So am I. I'll talk to you tomorrow, okay?" He kissed her again, lightly this time, as if aware of danger here.

Katy stared at the door after Jace closed it quietly behind him, and an astonishing thought blazed across her mind: she was falling in love with him.

She leaped back from that conclusion as quickly as she had plunged toward it. It was too soon for love, much too soon! She had known Jace only a few days, far too brief a time for any thought of *love*.

Yet she instantly stumbled over that sensible argument because, technically, it wasn't true. She *had* known him much longer. She shook her head, trying to clear her mind as her thoughts spiraled in a disorienting spin that tangled forgotten past and bewildering present.

Shakily she refilled the cup with lukewarm coffee and gulped it down.

The real problem was, she had known *herself* much too briefly.

Yet even as she steadied herself with that rational, level-headed conclusion, one truth burned through the logic and soared her spirits with sweet possibility: she *could* fall in love with Jace. Oh, yes, she could!

But a hard-reality phone call was about to come, one that would warn her against making any reckless leaps before she knew more about herself and her past.

Nine

Katy was in her bedroom when the phone rang. Mrs. L. was outside industriously weeding her small garden this morning, so Katy hobbled to the phone on the table beside the bed.

"May I speak to Kat, please?" A male voice, unfamiliar. Not surprising, she thought wryly, because almost no voice *was* familiar. A small frisson of excitement brought a dampness to her palms. Someone out of her past who knew her, who might jog her memory?

"This is Kat," she said, deciding not to bother explaining her small name alteration at the moment. She waited expectantly for him to identify himself.

But what she got was silence, then, "Kat?" spoken in that same incredulous tone that had crackled in Jace's voice the first time she spoke with him. "*Kat?*"

She found what was beginning to feel like a standard male reaction to her name more annoying than amusing. If he *was* calling her, why was he so astonished when she answered?

"Yes, Kat. And this is?"

"Your voice sounds odd."

She could explain that she'd been in an accident, or that last night's chilly escapade had left her with a scratchy throat. But with no idea who he was she instead said cautiously, "I'm sorry, I didn't catch your name?"

"C'mon, Kat, it's *Barry.*"

He sounded exasperated, as if he expected her to recognize not only the name but the voice as well, and she didn't recognize

101

either, of course. "Barry who?" she asked tentatively.

"Alexander, Kat. Barry *Alexander.*"

Her spine stiffened at his sarcastic tone, but perhaps it was justified if he was someone she should know and didn't. She didn't want to tell a stranger too much, and yet, from the way he spoke, he *wasn't* a stranger, and she had to offer some explanation. Cautiously, editing the situation down to skeletal facts, she said, "I'm sorry. I was in an accident recently, and sometimes things slip my mind."

"What kinds of things?" His voice changed, as if that information had suddenly wired it with electricity. She heard a small rustle of movement, perhaps a shifting of the phone to his other ear.

"Well, like who you are," she admitted.

"You don't remember *me?*"

"I'm sorry."

"Is this some kind of trick, Kat, pretending I'm someone you never heard of?" he demanded, suspicion now foremost in his voice. "Where have you been for the last few months?"

"No, it isn't a trick." Again, the similarity to Jace's reaction sent a shiver of surprise and uneasiness through her. Because she once *had* tried to trick Jace, of course, with her story about a prowler. Had she also done something unscrupulous to Barry Alexander? Warily she said, "I left the ranch to do some thinking, and I was in an accident and now I have a bit of a memory problem."

Charged silence, as if he were processing that through some mental maze. "How much of a problem? What *do* you remember?"

"Not much, actually," she admitted. Mrs. L. wouldn't approve, but Katy didn't like tap-dancing around the truth and abruptly decided simply to come out with the flat fact. "The doctor calls it amnesia. I don't remember anything."

"This accident, did it change your looks?"

The shallowness of the blunt question shocked her. She'd just admitted she had amnesia, couldn't even remember him, and he was concerned about her *looks?* "I do have this large, rather unflattering cast on my leg, but I assume it isn't permanently attached."

Another silence, this one not so much charged as puzzled by the tart comment. Then a tardy laugh, as if he finally realized she was being facetious or sarcastic.

"Okay, I'm coming out there, Kat."

"No!" she objected with instant alarm. "I don't want you to."

He ignored the rebuff. "I'll catch a flight to San Francisco later today and rent a car there, or get a commuter flight up to—what was the name of the town we flew into that other time?"

She dropped to the edge of the bed, surprised. "You've been here before?"

"Of course. We flew out together a few months before your parents were killed, shortly after you joined my agency. Oh, I remember now. Redding, that's the name of the town. But I'll probably arrive in the middle of the night, so I'll get a motel room and see you sometime tomorrow."

"Wait." He must have been a good friend if she'd brought him to the ranch, but she didn't *know* him, and she felt only panic at the idea of this disembodied voice descending on her. "Who *are* you? Where are you?"

He laughed, sounding at ease and comfortable now. "I'm in New York, of course, and I am, among other things, your fiancé."

He hung up, leaving her standing there staring at the phone.

She grabbed her crutches and clomped outside. Mrs. L. was kneeling beside a mound of tiny carrots she'd thinned from the row of feathery-green sprouts. The garden smelled of freshly turned damp earth, rich and fertile, but now Katy barely noticed the lush scents. She simply blurted out her question.

"Mrs. L., do I have a fiancé named Barry?"

Mrs. L. leaned back against her heels and with a gloved hand brushed a wisp of gray hair away from her nose. She looked up from beneath the floppy hat that shaded her eyes. "I don't know, sweetie. I suppose you could have. I believe a man named Barry came with you to visit your folks one time." She smiled. "But I have a hard time keeping track of your fiancés. After the second or third one I decided I wouldn't get excited until I actually saw you in a wedding gown." She paused reflectively. "Although, come to think of it, this Barry is probably the one who was here shortly before you left the ranch. And he called a time or two afterwards."

"He didn't mention being here a second time."

"Oh. Well, maybe I'm mistaken, then," she said vaguely. She added another handful of slender, golden orange carrots to the neat pile.

"He's coming again. He said he'd arrive tomorrow."

"He is?" Mrs. L. stood up and brushed dirt off her knees. She looked mildly alarmed. "Do you think that's wise, sweetie, letting him come here?"

"I didn't 'let him.' He said he was coming and hung up. What do you remember about him?"

Mrs. L. shook her head. "Not much. Tall and dark haired, I think. Good looking. They always are! He may have been a photographer or something like that."

"He said something about my joining his agency."

"Oh, Katy, this does worry me! If he's your fiancé, he's bound to know you well enough to see that you have memory problems, and if he spreads that gossip to people in the modeling business in New York—"

"Actually, he already knows," Katy admitted. "I had to tell him when I couldn't remember him on the phone. But he surely isn't going to spread gossip if he's my fiancé."

She stumbled over the word, feeling it collide with the bloom of her tentative new feelings for Jace. If she was engaged to Barry Alexander, she must be in love with *him*. Except that it was the woman she used to be, the old Kat Cavanagh, who was in love with Barry, of course. And *she* felt only an uneasy blend of curiosity and dismay at the prospect of his arrival.

Then another thought slammed into her, a shocking and appalling thought. Before her injuries, she was engaged to Barry Alexander. Yet she'd also tried to tempt Jace into a temporary fling. What kind of woman *was* she?

Jace and Joe came over that evening, with two boys whom Jace introduced as Mike and Ramsey from the school. Mike was a shy, big, redhead with freckles, Ramsey a small-for-his-age, African-American boy with a wooden earring and a mischievous smile.

All four males gathered around the disabled convertible as if it were some fabulous, newfound treasure, and words such as *carburetor* and *air cleaner* and *battery terminals* drifted up from the four heads bent under the raised hood. Greasy hands occasionally reached for tools on the nearby workbench, and once Ramsey, in spite of the slight limp with which he walked, slid with youthful agility under the car. Katy, sitting on the steps that descended from the house to the concrete floor of the garage, appreciated their rapt involvement in her vehicle's problems, but she also had a grumpy suspicion that *she* could have been wallowing in pneumonia after the chilly escapade and they wouldn't have been nearly as concerned or interested.

Although once Jace did glance up and give her a friendly wink.

The heads finally emerged, and Joe slid into the driver's seat to turn the key. The engine roared to life and purred smoothly. After a few more minutes correcting the problem with the stubborn convertible top, Joe pronounced the vehicle good as new. Katy lumbered to her feet, never a graceful procedure.

"Thanks, to all of you," she said, making sure to include the two budding young mechanics. "And what do I owe you?"

"Coffee or milk and more pie?" Jace suggested.

"I wasn't in a pie-making mood today, but Mrs. L. always has some of her marvelous cookies on hand."

The men and boys trooped inside and, because of their generally greasy aura, stood to gulp the cookies and drinks, filling the kitchen with a rich masculinity, scents of grease and oil, and more talk on mechanical subjects. When they started out the back way, Katy touched Jace's arm and asked if she could talk to him for a minute. He stayed behind while the others went on.

"I hope you didn't mind my bringing the boys along. We don't have a formal mechanics training program, but we try to help the boys develop their individual interests whenever we can."

"Bringing them along was fine."

"Would you like to go to the river with us again in a day or two?"

Katy didn't give her news any preliminary small talk. She just blurted it out. "Jace, I just found out today that I have a fiancé."

"You do?" Jace blinked in surprise and took a step backward, as if suddenly on guard.

"I never mentioned him?"

"No."

She ruefully filled in his unspoken thoughts. "But just

106

because I didn't tell you about him doesn't mean he didn't exist. Mrs. L. says he was here not long before I left the ranch."

"Could be. I wouldn't necessarily have known he was here if he arrived after our wine-throwing incident."

"He's coming again. Tomorrow."

Two crease lines formed between Jace's heavy brows, but his comment was carefully noncommittal. "That should be interesting."

"Sometimes I feel as if I've blundered into someone else's body and life, like some weird science-fiction story! I'm engaged to him, and I don't even know him. What am I going to do?"

Jace put his arms around her, but with much more caution than when he had kissed her the night before. It was a friendly gesture of comfort, no more. He was, she knew, recognizing the fact that if she had a fiancé, the situation between them was considerably changed. "Don't panic. Maybe seeing him will be just what you need to bring everything back to you."

"I'm not sure I want to remember everything! From what I know so far, I don't think I like myself very well. I don't appear to be a particularly admirable person. Who knows what kind of man I might be engaged to!"

Jace didn't argue that point. But his arms tightened fractionally when he said almost roughly, "If he causes problems or gives you any trouble, you call me, okay?"

She leaned back and smiled up at him, still apprehensive but not so panicky. "Okay. I appreciate that. Thank you."

Katy planted herself in a chair with a clear view of the driveway. A cool dampness from a night of rain hung in the air, and clouds still lingered low in the sky. She nervously flipped through an old *Ladies Home Journal* with her mother's name on the mailing label, then a *McCalls*, without really seeing either. About eleven o'clock a white, midsize car pulled into the driveway.

She watched, too curious not to be fascinated as the man slid out of the car. Her *fiancé*. Tall and dark haired, as Mrs. L. had said. And yes, definitely very good looking. Angular face, tanned complexion, deep-set eyes. His build was long-torsoed and lean rather than ruggedly brawny like Jace's. He closed the car door almost cautiously and paused with an odd alertness, as if sniffing for danger as he inspected the house and surrounding meadow and forest. He wore gray slacks and a black turtleneck, and there was an air of urban sophistication about him as he moved toward the house. A man who'd feel comfortable in a ritzy restaurant with a haughty maitre d' and with a woman who liked limousines and two-hundred-dollar haircuts. Was it something to do with him, she wondered, that triggered that I've-forgotten-something-vital feeling that still nagged her?

She opened the front door when he reached the deck. He stopped short when he saw her, as if he'd just slammed into an invisible wall.

By now Katy had lost much of her self-consciousness about her lack of hair and seldom thought about it. But with Barry staring at her she was acutely aware that it was still little more than a see-through veil of blond velvet on her scalp. And the last time he'd seen her she'd had that lush golden mane of the magazine photos.

"Kat, you didn't tell me! I know you said you were in an accident and had your leg in a cast, but you didn't say anything about *this*." He gestured accusingly toward the missing mane. "It'll take *years* to grow out." He sounded stunned, aghast, as if the lack of hair made her something less than a whole woman.

"I guess this gives new meaning to the phrase *having a bad hair day*, doesn't it?" she snapped.

He stopped short in the process of circling her as if she were some defective new species, and Katy had the strangest desire to laugh because *he* obviously had all the sense of humor of a frozen-faced male mannequin. Belatedly, he finally smiled. "I'm sorry. It was just something of a shock." He reached out, apparently intending to take her hands in his but couldn't because she gripped the crutches fiercely. He cupped his palms over her shoulders instead. "How are you, Kat?"

She resisted a desire to step away. This was, after all, her *fiancé*. "Katy," she corrected. "I go by the name of Katy now."

"Kat…Katy…you honestly don't remember me, not even when I'm standing right here?" His dark eyes probed hers as if trying to see beneath the blue.

"No. I'm sorry." She wanted to know how long he intended to stay, but it seemed rude to come right out and ask. She detoured the direct question by asking tentatively, "Do you have a suitcase or overnight bag?"

"Yes, of course. I'll run out to the car in a minute and get it."

Which meant he intended to stay longer than a midday lunch. She swallowed and rushed into something that she was determined to get out of the way immediately, before any awkward misunderstandings arose.

"Barry, I don't know what kind of relationship we had in the past." She paused, determined, but flustered with the prospect of having to plunge into details because he was looking at her so blankly. "I mean, I don't know how…intimate our relationship was.…"

The blank look lasted only a moment longer, and then she had to give him credit for a certain amount of insight. He might be short on sense of humor, but he wasn't totally insensitive or obtuse. "Of course. I understand perfectly."

Which was a relief, even though it didn't set her mind at ease about what their prior relationship may have been.

He carried his suitcase in from the car, and Mrs. L. showed him to an upstairs bedroom. He returned a few minutes later, dark hair freshly damp from a quick shower, and sat beside Katy on the ivory leather sofa. He smiled, a white flash that was as handsomely impressive as his angular face.

"I don't know quite what to say, since you don't remember me."

"I suppose we need to get acquainted all over again?"

"Yes! Exactly." He picked up her left hand and caressed her taut knuckles lightly with his fingertips, his eyes holding hers. Then, apparently feeling something amiss, he glanced down. "Kat, where's your ring?"

"Ring?"

"Your engagement ring!"

"I don't know," she admitted. Briefly she sketched the circumstances under which she'd been found, injured and without identification, on the Oregon beach. "There's a possibility that I may have been attacked and robbed and then dumped on the beach. Mrs. L. says I was probably carrying a fair amount of cash."

"And wearing a three-carat diamond ring!"

"I'm sorry." She suddenly felt guiltily careless about losing something so valuable, guilty about not remembering she'd ever worn such a ring, guilty about not remembering him and feeling only uneasiness with his nearness. This was her *fiancé.*

"The ring doesn't matter." His hands closed over hers, bending her fingers against her palm. "All that matters is that you're here and safe." He lifted her hand to his lips and tenderly kissed the empty ring finger. "A ring is replaceable. You aren't."

But the missing ring was more reason than ever to believe robbery had been the motive for what had happened to her.

Missing money, missing ring; it added up.

He suddenly looked stricken, as if the same thought had just occurred to him. "I hate to think that the ring may have been the *cause* of all this! But it would have been a terrible temptation to someone unscrupulous, of course."

Did she *know* unscrupulous people? Katy wondered uneasily. Or had it been a chance encounter with a stranger?

"Look, the ring doesn't matter," Barry said firmly. "We'll get another one. What's important is, as you said a minute ago, that we get reacquainted."

Reluctantly she finally said, "You might begin by telling me about our relationship."

"We've been engaged a little over a year." He kept a firm hold on her hand as he spoke, as if afraid she might disappear again. "We met when I photographed you on a swimsuit shoot in the Caribbean. You were with the Carlson modeling agency at that time, but when I opened my own agency, Alexander Models, you saw the possibilities and decided to join me. Later, after we became engaged, we flew out here together so I could meet your parents. Who were wonderful people, by the way. But you don't remember them either?"

Katy shook her head. "Mrs. L. said you were here another time, shortly before I left the ranch?"

She felt a jerky tightening of his fingers, but his voice was smooth when he said, "Yes, that's right. I needed your signature on a spectacular new contract as model and spokeswoman for a cosmetics company." He smiled. "And I was missing you desperately anyway, so it seemed a good reason to fly out."

"But, from what I've been able to figure out, I'd apparently decided to quit modeling and not return to New York. I had Mrs. L. ask my roommates to ship all my belongings out here."

He shook his head vigorously. "Oh, no, you weren't quitting modeling. We had this marvelous townhouse lined up to live in after we were married, but it was being remodeled and you couldn't move your things into it yet. So you decided you'd just have everything shipped out here."

That seemed an odd course of action, but, as Katy was often discovering, her pre-amnesia thought processes were not necessarily clear to her now.

"Your roommates…" He paused and then, with a certain delicacy, selected a tactful phrasing. "They were envious of your success in coming with my new agency, perhaps even a bit vindictive, and you were anxious to move on and get away from them."

That assessment of her roommates sounded plausible to Katy, given the carelessly packed condition of her belongings. "What happened on the contract with the cosmetics company?"

"When you seemed to disappear into thin air, they canceled. But don't worry. We'll come up with something even better."

"Not soon, I suspect." Katy instinctively fingered the skimpy tuft trying to curl in front of her ear. "I'm not exactly model material at the moment."

Barry leaned back and studied her appraisingly. "I'm thinking about that."

Mrs. L. appeared in the arched doorway and announced that lunch was ready. Barry jumped up from the leather sofa and solicitously helped Katy with her crutches. Mrs. L. served lunch in the dining room rather than the breakfast nook, where Katy usually ate when alone. Barry turned surprisingly entertaining as the two of them ate salad, chicken sandwiches, and iced tea, relating bits of spicy gossip and news from New York. Katy had no memory of the people he mentioned, but his little anecdotes were amusing anyway, and he seemed pleased to hear her laugh.

"Kat…" he began.

"Katy," she corrected.

"Katy, I hate to get back to troublesome matters, but do your doctors give you any idea when your memory may return?" He spoke as if she must have a team of experts working on this problem.

She offered him Dr. Fischer's earlier assessment. "Maybe soon. Maybe never."

"I see." He paused reflectively. "It doesn't really matter, of course. You're still tall and slim and elegantly beautiful. Whether you remember the past is irrelevant. It's the future that matters. And we can build a fantastic future for you. For us."

She laughed and stretched a wisp of hair to its skimpy limits. "With this?"

"I admit it was a shock when I first saw you, and I apologize for my insensitive reaction. The fact is, of course, that your hair will grow back, and we could get a wardrobe of wigs for you until then. But I think we should simply take advantage of the way things are. This is a fantastic opportunity for you to head in a totally new direction with a complete new persona."

"What do you mean?"

"An entirely new look for you, Kat. What you are now is different, striking, attention getting!" His hand hovered over her head like a caressing halo, not quite touching the blond velvet. "We'll create a whole new image for you. Sleek and haughty and aristocratic, disdainful of women who need *hair* to make them beautiful. We'll get that great new makeup artist Leticia to create a dramatic new look for your face. Kat, it'll be absolutely fantastic! We'll have every high-fashion magazine editor and trendy advertiser in the country begging for you."

Katy just sat there trying to keep her mouth from dropping open. Until this moment, during the times she'd vaguely tried to peer into her future, the idea of going back to modeling in

New York had not seemed a viable possibility. It simply wasn't *real*. But Barry not only seemed to think it was real and possible, he saw a glittering, rising-star future for her!

Ten

That evening, as they sat on the sofa with the sound turned down on the TV, Barry expanded on the possibilities, and Katy found herself peering into a glittering world of glamour and excitement. Her dramatic, shorn, "new look" face on magazine covers, a cosmopolitan life in a New York townhouse, lunches at elegant restaurants, interviews on television, perhaps hostess of her own show or a movie career before long! He dangled it all like a shimmering hologram, with an iridescent spotlight targeted on *her.*

"You don't seem particularly excited about any of this," he finally grumbled lightly when she sat there without responding.

"Actually, I'm quite dazzled. I don't know what to say. It's all rather breathtaking."

He turned on the sofa to face her, his tone suddenly urgent. "Come back to New York with me, Kat. *Now.* We can be married here before we leave, or as soon as we get back to New York. Whatever you want. But I don't want to leave you here alone."

"I'm not *alone,*" she protested.

"I want you with me. Without a memory, I'm afraid for you. Someone might try to take advantage of you. Please, come with me."

Katy swallowed. "I'll have to think about it. Right now, I just don't feel I can make any critical decisions."

"I understand. But I love you, Kat. Just remember that."

He leaned over to kiss her, but at the last moment she

dodged his lips, and the kiss landed on her cheek. She felt his body stiffen, but then he patted her arm reassuringly.

"That's okay. I know I still feel like a stranger to you. But we'll work things out."

The future prospects he offered *were* quite dazzling, she reflected as she lay in bed later. What girl wouldn't be drawn to the glamorous life he offered? Yet here in the dark bedroom, outside the glittering web he'd spun, some of the glow of enchantment dimmed. Was this really what she wanted to do with her life? It was what she'd done in the past, but wasn't there a certain shallowness to dedicating her life to using her face and body to sell shampoo and perfume and overpriced clothes?

She sat up and pulled aside the heavy drapery at the window beside the bed. From here she couldn't see the dark buildings or yard lights of Damascus, only the wild beauty of the moonless night. The meadow shimmering in faint starlight, the forest dark and silent, the snowy mountain gleaming in silver and shadows. Above, each star glittered like a diamond tossed on midnight velvet, undimmed by city lights or urban haze. All so beautiful that it brought an ache to her throat.

A small click of the phone jolted her out of her drifting reverie of the beauty of the night, the sound unnaturally large in the dark silence of the bedroom. Her hand tightened around the fold of drapery. The tiny sound was nothing, of course. Some peculiarity of the phone hookup made this phone give that tiny click whenever another phone in the house was used. It only meant Mrs. L. or Barry was dialing out. The hour was late for a call, but there was nothing unusual or odd about it. And yet…

For no reason an inexplicable uneasiness flickered through

her. She tried to examine the feeling with detached logic. *Why* did she feel uneasy? Perhaps because she didn't quite believe Barry's dazzling visions of the future? Perhaps because here, outside the golden circle he drew around them as a couple, his talk about the glamour and success of life with him in New York sounded just a bit like the spiel of a used-car salesman trying to sell a shiny sports car with a fatal defect in the transmission?

Yes, there was that. Yet there was more. She stared out the window at the moonless night again, and a strange, otherworldly feeling drifted around her, an eerie aura of unreality. Yes, the stars and forest and mountain were real enough, but here in this man-made house, reality wavered, like a reflection in water disturbed by a ripple of waves, or a photograph just a little out of focus.

She shivered, not from cold but from a sudden jolt of fear.

She instantly scoffed at the electric jolt. Fear? What was there to fear? That someone might "take advantage of her," as Barry suggested? Who? Or perhaps what she really felt was a certain apprehension about Barry himself? She pondered that possibility briefly but abandoned it. His visions of glamour and success might be overblown, but there was nothing to *fear* from him.

Yet the unfocused fear lingered, gathering out of the darkness like some noxious cloud enveloping her. A fear of something unknown, of illusions and secrets shivering behind the glossy facade of her life, mysteries lurking in the empty pit of her past.

The phone rang, and she jumped, suddenly afraid to answer it. But she must answer it, of course. The other phones in the house would also ring and could waken someone. She raised up on one elbow and fumbled for the instrument in the darkness.

"Hello?" she said cautiously.

"Did I wake you? The lights in the house are out, but I can't see your bedroom window from here, and I was worried about you." Jace broke off awkwardly as if it had suddenly occurred to him he could be intruding on some intimate reunion.

She dropped to the pillow in relief at the sound of his familiar, husky voice and cradled the receiver against her ear. "I wasn't asleep. And I'm glad you called." So very glad!

"Is something wrong, Katy?" Jace asked sharply. "I saw him arrive. Is he giving you a bad time or upsetting you?"

"No. Everything is fine. I was just lying here having an attack of nerves, I guess."

"Prewedding jitters?" he asked lightly.

"No!" Less vehemently, but no less positively, she added, "Definitely no plans for a wedding. In fact, it seems that somewhere along the way I lost his engagement ring. Do you remember my wearing it?"

"No." His unspoken thought lingered, and she couldn't deny the ugly possibility. Perhaps she had simply removed the ring around Jace so he wouldn't know she was engaged. He jumped to a less loaded subject. "Is he bringing back memories?"

"Not a one."

A small silence and then Jace said awkwardly, "Well, I'll let you go, then. I didn't call to pry. I was just concerned about you."

"No, don't go yet! Please." Jace was solid reality, no deceptive facade or secrets here. "It feels reassuring to talk to you."

"Reassuring?"

"He wants me to come back to New York with him. Along with being engaged to him, I'm a model with his agency. He thinks my 'new look' could be a big success."

"I don't know anything about the fashion or advertising business, but I suppose that could be true. Is that what you want to do?"

"I don't know," she admitted.

"How do you feel about him, Katy?"

"As owner of the modeling agency or as my fiancé?"

"Whatever." She heard a deliberate shrug in the word, as if he didn't want to admit a personal concern if she was madly in love with Barry.

She searched through the maze of impressions and reactions that had accumulated during the day. A little lamely she finally said, "He seems nice."

Unexpectedly Jace laughed, a husky chuckle holding honest amusement. "I would hope, if I'm ever engaged, that my beloved has something more dynamic than 'he seems nice' to say about me."

She had to laugh with him at her insipid statement. "But I must have been in love with him or I wouldn't be engaged to him?" An unplanned upswing made a question of what she had thought was a statement.

"People change. Feelings change." He hesitated and then added lightly, "You've changed. And my feelings about you have changed."

"I still don't share your spiritual faith."

"No. But God is working on you."

Katy strongly doubted that. If there was a higher power, she still felt abandoned, not worked on, by him. But she was sure of something else. "I'm glad you called," she said with husky sincerity.

He hesitated and then said softly, "So am I. And remember, if you need me, I'm here. And so is the Lord."

She replaced the phone and snuggled back under the covers.

The odd feeling of unreality had receded now, fading like an unpleasant dream, and with it went that inexplicable fear. Solid, steady Jace was there. She could count on Jace.

Next morning after breakfast Mrs. L. reminded her that her appointment with the doctor in Yreka was that afternoon, and Barry offered to drive her to it.

"I don't want to put you to all that trouble," Katy protested. "You'd have to drive back here again instead of going on to catch your plane."

Barry smiled. "You're not rushing me off to a plane just yet, my dear Kat. I intend to take you back to New York with me when I go."

She detoured the New York issue. "I wish you'd call me Katy."

"Katy doesn't really fit the dramatic, ultrasophisticated image I want to project for you."

"I don't feel ultrasophisticated. I'm not sure I want to *be* ultrasophisticated."

Barry simply laughed indulgently, as if she were acting like a sulky child.

On the almost two-hour drive on the rough, winding road to Yreka, Katy questioned him about her career and her personal life in New York. He told her about photographic shoots they'd been on together, parties they'd attended, even little squabbles they'd had, but everything was as foreign as if she were reading it for the first time in a novel.

The doctor examined and x-rayed her leg through the cast, said everything looked good and that he should be able to remove the cast in another three weeks. On the drive home it was Barry's turn to ask questions about everything that had happened in the last few weeks. He also probed gently at the blankness before that. Katy was tired by the time they got home and excused herself for a nap. She wandered out to the kitchen when she woke.

"Where's Barry?" she asked.

"He said he was going for a walk. I think he headed toward the river." Mrs. L. opened the oven door and expertly added a smidgen of garlic to the roast already sending out savory scents.

"Somehow he doesn't seem like a walk-in-the-woods sort of person," Katy mused, although she remembered he had mentioned working out at his health club. She snagged a freshly toasted crouton from a tray on the stove and crunched appreciatively. "He wants me to go back to New York with him, as you heard. He thinks I can start working again as soon as the cast comes off, perhaps even before."

"That may be just what you need."

Katy's hand stopped in surprise as she reached for another crouton. She'd expected Mrs. L. to raise a protective fuss if Katy even thought about leaving the ranch again so soon.

"Katy, I think he loves you and has your best interests at heart. I think you should go back to New York with him and get into the swing of the life you loved there."

"But if I'd already decided to leave that life, maybe I didn't love it." She hesitated. "Did my parents like Barry?"

"Why, yes, I believe they did."

"But I can't marry him if I can't remember him!"

"Katy, you have to consider the strong possibility that you aren't going to remember, that you just have to go on from where you are now," Mrs. L. said gently. "You can still have a wonderful life even if you never remember, and going back to modeling as soon as possible can get you started on it."

"That's true, you know."

Neither of them had heard Barry come in, and both jumped at the sound of the unexpected male voice. He was in his stocking feet, his muddy shoes held at arm's length from his body. Katy had to laugh in spite of being startled. He was regarding the shoes as if mud were some hazardous contaminant.

"Where in the world did you walk?" Katy asked. She hadn't seen dark, gooey mud like that when Jace took her back to the river.

"I got into some mucky place out in the woods. I'm a city boy," he added with a good-humored laugh. "With my sense of direction it's a wonder you didn't have to send out a pack of search dogs to sniff me out."

After dinner the two of them played Scrabble, Katy winning easily, which she found frustrating. How come she could remember a word such as *egalitarian* but couldn't remember this good-looking, laughing guy who said he loved her?

He stayed on, going through photograph albums with her the next day, turning back his cuffs and getting an endearing smudge of flour on his face when he rolled out pie crust for her, helping Mrs. L. weed the garden while Katy looked on, pulling out a camera and snapping shots of her at unexpected moments. He even tenderly gave her a pedicure one evening, laughing as he carefully if inexpertly applied a shimmery pink to her toenails peeking out from beneath the cast.

But on the third day, she unexpectedly collided with a totally different side of him.

Eleven

The hour was early, not yet seven A.M. Katy had just taken a semishower and sponge bath. Oh, how glad she'd be when she could soak in the tub for an hour! She was struggling clumsily into shorts when she impulsively decided to call Dr. Fischer and report on her doctor's appointment. At this hour, she could catch the doctor at home, before hospital rounds.

She picked up the phone, and the ugly, threatening words spewing from it like verbal sewage rammed shock waves through her.

She was so astonished that rather than instantly replacing the phone as common courtesy and respect for privacy demanded, she simply held it a foot away from her ear as the harsh blast about some unpaid bill or loan continued. Barry finally interrupted with a raw curse of his own and added tightly, "You'll have your money. I paid up before, didn't I? Business couldn't be better, and I'm working on something big now." He sounded angry and scornful, but Katy also heard a note of bluff or bluster in his voice, plus a raw undercurrent of fear.

"Don't try to con us, Alexander," the rough voice retorted. "We are *not* happy with this. And you know how unpleasant things can get when we're unhappy."

Katy replaced the receiver quietly and glanced at the clock. It would be almost ten o'clock in New York now, which was where he'd probably placed the call to this person to whom he owed money. Loan shark? The term leaped out of that fund of general knowledge that frustratingly excluded her personal past. And a question also leaped out and landed like a hard fist in the pit of her stomach. Was *she* the 'something big' he was working on?

She expected him to come downstairs looking agitated and worried, but he was his usual affable, charming self over breakfast, giving no hint that he'd just been cursed and threatened. Katy was still in shock over the ugly phone conversation, but she couldn't ask him about it, of course, nor could she challenge him about the 'something big' he was working on. But Barry was observant enough to notice that she rearranged rather than ate her scrambled eggs.

"Something wrong this morning?" he inquired as he refilled the coffee cup she'd already nervously emptied twice.

She evaded a direct answer. "I guess I didn't sleep well."

He reached across the table and tilted her downturned chin up. "That's because you need a loving husband to hold you in the night and chase away bad dreams," he whispered with a teasing smile. "Kat...Katy...let's get married today."

"*Today?*"

"No waiting time required in Nevada! We'll drive over to Reno, have a quick ceremony, honeymoon in the bright lights for a couple of days, and then fly back to New York." Persuasively he stroked the side of her throat with his fingertips. "I do have to get home, hon. It's been wonderful here, but New York is where the action is. For both of us."

If she'd been tempted to go back to New York with him before, the overheard phone conversation made her reconsider. In fact, even though she felt guilty adding to whatever difficulties he already faced, there was something she had to do.

"I'm sorry, Barry, but I can't just jump into marrying you." She swallowed before determinedly rushing on. "In fact, under the circumstances, I think we should consider our engage—"

He crossed her lips with a finger to shush her. "No! I won't let you say it." His voice was agitated but tender. "Kat, you aren't being fair! Don't you owe me more than tossing me out like an old shoe?"

His passionate plea brought her up short. *Was* she being unfair? Did she owe him more? The questions rattled her but didn't change her mind.

"Barry, I can't marry you! I don't even *know* you!" Truly an understatement, she thought with a shiver. "And I'm not sure I want to return to modeling."

"You can't mean that! I've already lined up new assignments so you can start work immediately when you return to New York."

"You shouldn't have done that without consulting me!"

His mouth compressed into a hard line, and the angry flicker in his eyes surprised her. And told her she was correct in her suspicion that she was the "something big" he was counting on to extricate him from his troubles. The tender caress along her throat turned to a hard brush of knuckles, and for a moment she had the horrified impression that he was going to draw back his fist and strike her. She jerked back, neck stiff, shocked eyes riveted on him.

Then his hand slid around to cup the nape of her neck gently, and she felt guilty about the brief, unfair suspicion.

"Kat, you're not the kind of woman to sit out here in the sticks and rot! You're too smart, too beautiful." He smoothed a wisp of hair at her temple and smiled affectionately. "And as stubborn as ever, of course. Same old infuriating Kat, even with your memory gone, aren't you? Although sweeter now. Yes, definitely sweeter."

Kat twisted the coffee cup in a nervous corkscrew of circles, uncertain how to react to this abrupt switch from tenderness to fury and back to tenderness.

"We'll put our engagement on hold, if that makes you more

comfortable. But I can't accept that it's ended, Kat. I *won't* accept that."

An engagement "on hold" sounded meaningless to Katy, but she was suddenly too anxious for Barry to leave to argue details. He hadn't actually *done* anything, and perhaps she was being unfair, but tension and apprehension about the web of personal and career entanglements he was trying to tighten around her still throbbed in her rigid neck muscles.

Barry left later that day. He kissed her on the cheek and said he'd call in a few days. She felt like kicking herself that she'd allowed the status of their relationship to be so imprecise, because as far as she was concerned, the engagement was *over.* But she had, at least, convinced him not to express-mail another ring out to her.

She called Jace that evening. He came over, and they sat on the front deck in the meadow-scented dusk and sipped iced tea as the stars came out. They talked about the last few days, although Katy reluctantly knew she couldn't tell him about that disturbing phone call. The fact that she'd *listened* was bad enough; she certainly couldn't reveal to someone else the contents of that private conversation.

"How do you feel about him now that he's gone back to New York?" Jace asked finally. She suspected he knew she wasn't telling him something.

"Relieved," Katy answered simply.

Jace smiled as if he approved her response. "Will *you* go back to New York eventually?"

Katy admitted her mixed feelings. "I don't know. Maybe. Maybe not."

"Being a well-known model is the dream of a lot of girls."

Yes. It had obviously been her dream once. But was it now?

They didn't spend all evening talking about Barry and modeling and New York, however. Some new boys had arrived for the summer session, and Jace was excited about them. One of the mares had a new foal. The school was on the verge of receiving a substantial corporate grant with which to buy new classroom computers. There'd been a smelly crisis when a skunk wandered into an open door of the dormitory.

She felt at ease with him. Secure. In an easy patch of wordless but comfortable companionship, the deep croak of a frog punctuated the chirpy music of night insects.

"It sounds as if there must be a million of them," Katy said idly.

"You mean the crickets?"

Katy slowly straightened her slouchy posture in the wooden deck chair. "Crickets?" she repeated.

"I think they make the sound by rubbing their legs together. Probably a mating call or maybe a territorial claim."

Katy wasn't interested in how the insects handled their communication or their love life. Yet a strange tingle shivered through her. Crickets. She repeated the word slowly. "Crickets." And again, almost wonderingly, *"Crickets."*

In the silvery starlight Jace peered at her curiously. "You've developed a sudden interest in bugs?"

Katy laughed. An interest in bugs? She, who had screeched when she encountered a quarter-inch, many-legged thing in the bathtub the other night? "No, I don't think so." She resumed her comfortable slouch in the wooden chair. Crickets surely didn't interest her. Yet the word inexplicably lingered, like a familiar echo inside her head. *Crickets.*

Before he left, Jace again invited her to Sunday services at the school, and this time she accepted.

127

~~~~~

She carefully held herself aloof from the message as she sat beside Jace that Sunday in the chapel sweetly scented with bouquets of the roses now in full bloom. She had come because she wanted to be with him, not because of some sudden softening in her resistance to the spiritual. When the chaplain called everyone to prayer she bowed her head with the others, but her thoughts were rebellious challenges, not submissive prayer: *Okay, God,* she demanded, *if you're out there and haven't forgotten me, where's my memory?*

Yet she reluctantly had to admit that the music almost got to her. Little Ramsey sang "God Will Take Care of You" with such sweet purity that she had to blink away tears. Why, she thought almost angrily, did it all feel so familiar? Why did it *call* to her? She was no believer naively trusting that God would take care of everything. She knew better!

The powerful question that followed that defiant claim made her hands curl rigidly around the hymnal. How did she "know better"?

Her thoughts hovered on the edge of the pit like a diver poised to plunge into dark waters. No dive came, but she refused to soften her unyielding stance simply because she couldn't answer the question. She just *knew,* that was all.

Yet her hostility toward the Lord didn't keep her from staying for dinner in the dining room. She met other members of the staff, plus the wives of two staff members who shared an apartment in Yreka during the week so they could hold jobs there. Both were older than Katy, but she welcomed the female contact. One small bit of awkwardness arose when one wife pointed out that she and Katy had met before and Katy couldn't remember her, of course. She was glad Jace had kept his promise not to tell anyone about her memory problems, but she also had the unhappy feeling she now came off looking like a New York snob who dismissed the locals as too insignificant to remember. Determined to erase that impression, she suggested lunch the next time she was in Yreka for a doctor's appointment. The woman, Shirley Edmundson, looked surprised but readily accepted and offered her apartment and work phone numbers.

He stood at the plate-glass window on the tenth floor, hands braced on the windowsill, deep carpet luxurious underfoot. But his thoughts were not on carpet or the view of tall buildings and slow-moving traffic in the urban canyons below. His thoughts were on Kat Cavanaugh.

Or, to be more accurate, on the woman who was a dead ringer for Kat Cavanaugh.

He turned, pulled the wallet from his hip pocket, and studied the small photo snapped when she was unaware of the camera. Wouldn't she be surprised, he thought with the twist of a smile, if she knew he carried it with him like a good-luck talisman?

He wouldn't have believed the similarity possible except for the concrete fact of her presence there on the ranch, if the amazing truth were not right here in this photo. Those same aristocratic cheekbones, those incredible blue eyes, those fantastic legs! Impossible. Yet it was true. She looked enough like the real Kat Cavanaugh to be her clone. The buzz-cut hair was a shocker, of course, but it was also an advantage because it drew attention away from any minor discrepancies. Not that there really were discrepancies, however. Maybe a few more pounds on her elegant frame, but they were in all the right places.

But there was her personality. Oh, yes, that was a difference, a huge difference. This one was actually nice, a word he doubted had ever been applied to the real Kat.

That first phone call had almost panicked him. He'd thought it couldn't possibly mean anything but big trouble. Who was she, anyway? What if someone came looking for her?

But now, in spite of today's latest wrench-in-the-works disaster, his confidence was running on high octane. He'd kept the financial problems hidden and had most people fooled, but things were not going as well as they looked on the surface, not by a long shot. The situation was, in fact, beginning to crumble and stink like a ball of rotten cheese.

But, for the moment anyway, he could stop worrying that some nosy busybody would initiate a search for the real Kat and maybe even turn up her body. So far as everyone now knew, Kat was right there at the ranch nursing a broken leg. In fact, he thought with a certain righteousness, if the real Kat Cavanaugh had been more like her substitute rather than the arrogant, deceitful, cruel, coldhearted, ruthlessly selfish, and ambitious barracuda she was—oh, the list could go on and on!—she might be alive today. And if this woman's memory never returned, he was home free!

Of course, if she did start to remember she wasn't Kat Cavanaugh...

He frowned. It would be harder this time. He wasn't gut-deep angry with this woman as he had been with the real Kat. But if it had to be done...

He clenched a fist and slammed it toward the window, toned muscles flexing as he stopped just short of ramming the fist through the plate glass. He could do it. Oh, yes, he could do it.

Twelve

The lunch with the two wives in Yreka happened sooner than Katy expected. Her cast developed a hairline crack near the ankle, and Mrs. L. drove her into Yreka on Thursday so the doctor could inspect it. He reinforced the cast with tape although he said he wasn't really concerned about it. The cast would be coming off soon. Freedom! Katy thought exultantly as she made the appointment for just two weeks away.

She phoned Shirley Edmundson and arranged to meet both her and the other woman, Alice Kelt, for lunch. Mrs. L. dropped Katy at the combination sandwich shop and antique store, promising to be back in an hour. Shirley and Alice were already at a small, circular table covered with a pink-checked cloth when Katy arrived. Antique kitchen implements decorated the walls, and an old-fashioned, cast-iron cookstove covered with potted geraniums filled one corner.

"I'm so glad you could both get away for lunch," Katy said after settling herself and the crutches. She felt a little awkward now that she was here. She suspected curiosity was the main reason the women had come. The waitress arrived, and hearing the specials and ordering sandwiches and drinks took up a few minutes.

"It was nice to see you in the chapel on Sunday," Shirley offered after the waitress departed. "I don't believe you've come before."

"No, but I very much admire the work everyone at Damascus is doing," Katy said. "Jace and Joe and a couple of the boys fixed my car after I had a problem with it."

"Yes, Jace is quite a guy." Alice smiled with surprising imp-ishness. "But we got the impression you'd already noticed that."

Katy felt the warmth of a blush. Were her blooming feelings for Jace that obvious?

"Don't mind my friend the incurable romantic here," Shirley said with a combination grimace and laugh. "After twenty years of marriage, she still makes her husband heart-shaped cakes on Valentine's Day."

"But it is nice that Jace seems to have something on his mind besides work, work, work," Alice said. "Although, with the school's current financial problems and all…"

"The school's always in a state of financial crisis," Shirley said wryly.

"This must be more than the usual problems. Hank said they've had to cut back on supplies. Didn't Tom tell you?"

Unexpectedly, both women looked at Katy, as if assuming she was close enough to Jace to have privileged information.

She shook her head, a little embarrassed at how little she did know. "I haven't even seen or heard from Jace since Sunday." She hesitated. "I've wondered if something was wrong over there."

To be more accurate, she'd wondered if something was wrong between Jace and her. Perhaps he'd thought one session in the chapel would turn her into a devoted believer and had been disappointed when she merely asked skeptical questions about the message.

"Oh, I don't think there's any real problem," Shirley said. "The Lord always comes through. Tom is expecting new class-room computers soon. You know how computers are out of date practically before the delivery truck arrives."

"Yes, I know," Katy said. She stopped short. She didn't

know anything about computers. Or did she?

For a breathless moment something edged up from within the pit and balanced on the brink of the darkness. She squeezed her hands into fists, willing the formless something to take shape. Almost...*almost!* Then the cheerful waitress plopped a man-sized sandwich piled thick with turkey breast and ham in front of her, and the dark pit swallowed everything again.

Katy felt almost limp with the effort and disappointment, but the lunch continued pleasantly with talk about Damascus and the two women's activities during the week here in Yreka. They asked curious questions about the life of a New York model, and Katy used secondhand information acquired from Barry to answer them. And she could answer in the affirmative one question put to her: yes, she knew Cindy Crawford. Barry had said so. Of course, she didn't admit that she couldn't now remember the supermodel. The lunch ended with the two women's encouragement for Katy to come to Sunday services again, and she promised she would.

On the way home Katy thought with frustration of that brief moment when an elusive *something* had almost emerged from the dark pit, with it the same shivery tingle she'd felt at the mention of crickets. Although probably none of it meant anything, she decided ruefully. Crickets and computers were hardly a logical or meaningful combination. And what did either have to do with the sophisticated life of a New York model?

Back home, Katy wondered if Jace had tried to call while she and Mrs. L. were gone. They didn't have an answering machine. One of her father's small peculiarities was that he hated the things and wouldn't have one in the house. She could get one now, of course. Not that she was deluged with phone calls even when she was home.

She made a cherry cobbler and fidgeted restlessly after dinner, uneasy that she hadn't heard from Jace all week. She was tempted to call him, but decided instead to complete the call to Dr. Fischer that she'd started to make when Barry was at the ranch. The doctor was delighted to hear from her, pleased that a date had been set for removal of the cast, sympathetic that in spite of Katy's tantalizing reaction to *crickets* and *computers,* no real memories had surfaced. The phone rang again immediately after Katy hung up, and she reached for it eagerly, hoping the caller was Jace.

The male voice was unfamiliar, however, and it asked for Mrs. Lennox.

"Just a moment. I'll get her."

"Wait. Is this Kat...Katy?"

"Yes."

"Katy! This is Evan. Mrs. Lennox's son." He hesitated and then added a little awkwardly, "I hope you don't mind, but Mom told me about your amnesia. I've thought about calling to talk to you, but I know you can't remember me, and I didn't want to make you uncomfortable."

Katy dropped to the edge of the bed, appreciating his consideration for her feelings. It was also nice, she thought wryly, to talk to a man who didn't greet her with "*Kat?*" in an incredulous tone of disbelief. "I don't know what I'd do without your mother. She's been my Rock of Gibraltar here."

"She is that, isn't she? Can I do anything to help?" She liked his voice, deeply masculine but warm and concerned.

"Yes. Talk to me," she said impulsively. Wasn't it said that sometimes old people got fuzzy about the present but could remember far in the past with unclouded clarity? Maybe that

134

was the way to attack her amnesia, with someone who'd shared her childhood memories as a child himself. She stretched out on the bed, free leg bent. "Tell me about when we were kids together."

"Well, let's see." He laughed, a chuckle as husky and pleasant as his voice. She remembered seeing snapshots of the two of them together, she tall and skinny, he, even though he was a couple of years older, shorter and more solid, with sturdy legs and a tousle of curly blond hair. "Do you want to hear about the nice things, such as the time we made sticky-sweet Mother's Day cards? Or about all the mischief we got into together, like the time we splattered the kitchen with globs of chocolate and strawberry in an ice-cream fight?"

"We didn't!"

"Oh, yes, we did. A fight which, I might add, you won. For a girl, you had a really wicked overhand throw," he teased. "Not that winning did you any good. We were both sentenced to cleaning up the mess."

He went on, telling her of other escapades they'd shared, how he'd helped her with math and she'd helped him with boring history stuff, how they'd learned to swim together, how good her parents always were to him. "That was before your mother started writing children's books, but she always made up these wonderful bedtime stories for us. They always treated me as if I were a member of the family, not just the housekeeper's son."

"It sounds as if we had a wonderful childhood together." And, Katy thought ruefully, as if she were a rather nicer person then than she'd grown up to be.

"But you don't remember any of it?"

"Nothing. I'm sorry. Evan, do you remember anything about crickets from when we were kids?" she asked suddenly.

"Crickets? No, I don't think so. Why?"

"I don't know. I just felt odd the first time I heard the word, as if maybe it had some special meaning for me."

"You hated bugs and creepy-crawly things, so I was always teasing you with them, of course. I remember putting some kind of bug in your bed once, maybe a cricket, and you ran out screaming like a banshee."

Katy laughed. "I hope I got back at you some way."

"I don't remember how just now, but I'm sure you did."

"Are you planning to come up to visit your mother soon?" She wished he would. Talking with him felt like a warm link with the past.

"Nothing definite planned right now, but I do a lot of traveling for the company, so you never know."

"Your mother says you work too hard. She wishes you'd settle down with a nice girl and provide her with some grandchildren." Even though she couldn't remember him, she felt old-friends comfortable with him, free to say something teasingly personal like that.

He laughed companionably. "Don't *you* start on me about that, too! Do you remember—no, of course you don't, I'm sorry. But you and I had kind of a thing going for a while when we were in high school. Mom wasn't working for your folks by then, and you and I went to different schools, but we hung out together anyway. I had this big, bad motorcycle and a black leather jacket, and you liked to roar around with me." He laughed again. "But I guess we both outgrew that adolescent foolishness."

They talked a little longer, and then Katy put the phone down and went to tell Mrs. L. that Evan was on the line. Mrs. L. was meticulously cleaning the stove after a minor spill while cooking dinner, and she looked a little flustered as she dropped her scouring pad.

"Oh, my, I usually call him. It isn't up to you to be answering phone calls for *me.*"

"He can call anytime," Katy assured her. "We had a wonderful chat about old times. I loved talking with him. And he's certainly welcome to come visit anytime."

After Mrs. L. finished talking with Evan, a thought, perhaps aroused by Evan's reference to her mother's storytelling, occurred to Katy. "Mrs. L., how did my mother write her books?"

"How? Why, I don't know, sweetie. I guess she just had this wonderful imagination."

"No, I mean how *physically.* Longhand? typewriter? computer?"

"Oh, *how.* At first she wrote every word in pen on a yellow legal pad, but she switched to a computer several years ago. It's upstairs in her studio."

"I'm going up there!"

"Oh, Katy, you could so easily fall on the stairs!"

"Not the way I'm going to do it."

Katy hobbled to the foot of the stairs, handed her crutches to Mrs. L., plunked herself down on the third step and, using her hands and one good leg, scooted her bottom upwards step by step, a method that was effective if somewhat lacking in grace and elegance. She'd probably have figured out how to do this earlier, she realized, but getting upstairs hadn't seemed important until now. Now she wanted to get her hands on that computer.

Yet once she was seated at the computer, with her leg awkwardly propped to one side, no magic revelations about how to use it came to her. She tentatively pushed a couple of control buttons, but the dead screen showed only a faint reflection of her own face.

"Maybe it's unplugged," Mrs. L. suggested.

Katy laughed delightedly. Of course! The first lesson in computers. Always make sure the computer is plugged in before you panic and call the repairman.

Mrs. L. got down on her hands and knees and fumbled with the cord. A tiny bulb on the surge protector glowed red, and the machine itself whispered small internal noises, as if gently waking after a long hibernation. Then color sprang to the screen, and Katy's fingers felt an odd little tingle of excitement.

"There's probably an instruction book somewhere. Mavis would never throw something like that away." Mrs. L. peered into drawers and came up with an imposing array of manuals on various software programs. She shook her head. "I'm going back to my kitchen now. No one is ever going to convince me that computers aren't just some sort of electronic voodoo."

How to use the computer didn't all come back to Katy in a glorious rush of expertise, but after skimming manuals and tentatively pressing keys and sliding the mouse around, she began to feel a definite sense of familiarity. She stumbled into a game of solitaire, found a colorful array of graphics and a travel guide, and got chastised with a couple of error messages. Oh, and there was a word processing program, with a long menu of file names! Katy selected one that matched the name of one of her mother's books, and there, direct from her mother's imagination to the computer screen, was the story of how red-haired LuAnn conquered the monsters in her closet.

She wandered further, feeling more confident with each changing flash of the screen. Letters from her mother to an editor, notes to small readers who had written her, plot ideas, all of it making Katy feel closer than ever before to this mother she couldn't remember. Her father had used the computer, too, because there were letters to firms with which he did business, fiery missives to politicians with whom he disagreed, a complaint to the Forest Service about over-logging. Oh, and here were financial records, neatly kept current daily. Until stopping with abrupt finality one day last summer.

Katy was ready to shut the computer off then, suddenly tired and a little depressed, but one more item caught her eye. It was a letter written to her parents' lawyer outlining several changes they wanted in their wills. Most were simply to clarify Katy's position in regard to contracts her father had with various companies, but Mrs. L. was also mentioned. The name didn't surprise Katy, but the amount of the bequest did: $100,000. She stared at the number, puzzled. That certainly didn't jibe with the very modest sum Mrs. L. had available in her checking account when she made a partial payment on Katy's hospital bill and which she'd said was an inheritance from Katy's parents.

Katy felt gratified knowing her parents had intended to be generous with Mrs. L., and perhaps Mrs. L. had most of the money securely tucked away in an investment account somewhere. But was it possible this letter had not been sent before her parents' deaths, and Mrs. L. thus hadn't received the amount she should have?

After shutting off the computer, Katy slid her crutches down the stairs and cautiously made her own slower, bottom-sliding descent to the main floor. Mrs. L. had gone to her room, but a crack of light showed beneath the door.

Mrs. L. opened the door when Katy knocked, and Katy realized she'd never seen inside the room before. It was a homey clutter of plants, piles of quilting squares, sewing machine, stacks of magazines and tiny TV, with the cats sprawled on the bed. Framed photos and a bulletin board of smaller snapshots covered most of one wall.

"That's my Evan, of course," Mrs. L. said proudly when she

saw Katy looking at the photos. "Would you like to come in and see?"

The wall held a lifetime of Evan: Evan cherubic as a sturdy blond boy, smoldering and rebellious as a long-haired teenager, impressively handsome as an adult standing beside a gleaming, low-slung car.

Mrs. L. pointed to an eight-by-ten photo of Evan, formally attired in a dark suit, shaking hands at a podium with an older man. "That's when he won a company award for setting up the most new franchises. And these are when he was on vacation in Hawaii." She unpinned several snapshots from the bulletin board and handed them to Katy.

Evan was impressively muscular in swim trunks, superbly athletic on a surfboard, mischievously sexy leaning against a palm tree with a flowered lei around his neck. "No wonder you're so proud of him," Katy said honestly. She smiled. "Would it be rude to say he's gorgeous?"

Mrs. L.'s beaming smile said that wouldn't be rude at all. "Oh, and this one! It's you and Evan when you were children, playing in a wading pool together."

It was a photo Katy had seen before in one of the family albums. Katy posing prettily, already showing her height, sturdy-bodied Evan industriously scooping up water with a pail. Probably getting ready to dump it on her, Katy thought with a smile.

"Does it bring anything back to you?" Mrs. L. sounded wistful.

Katy shook her head regretfully as she handed back the snapshots and returned to the reason she'd knocked. "I was wandering around in the computer files."

"You figured out how to run it, then?"

"Unlikely as it seems, using a computer almost felt familiar."

"After you went up to the studio, I remembered that your

mother showed you how to work it one time when you were here. You spent a lot of time on it, as I recall."

"That probably explains why it felt so familiar. Anyway, in one of the files I found some information that indicated you should have received a fairly generous sum from my parents' estate."

"Oh, I did! Very generous."

"Forgive me, I don't mean to pry." Katy paused, embarrassed because she *was* prying. "But earlier you seemed, well, a little strapped financially."

Mrs. L. stopped short in the act of pinning the snapshots on the bulletin board, and for one uneasy moment Katy thought she was going to retort that her finances were none of Katy's business. Instead Mrs. L. put her fingertips together and looked embarrassed herself.

"I know Thornton and Mavis left me the money because they wanted me to be secure financially if anything happened to them. But shortly after their deaths I learned my elderly aunt Cora, my only living relative besides Evan, desperately needed an organ transplant. It was considered an experimental procedure, so Medicare wouldn't pay for it, and, well, I couldn't just let her die without trying to help." Mrs. L. twisted her fingers together nervously.

"Did the transplant save her?"

Mrs. L. shook her head regretfully. "She died anyway."

"But you'd have felt even worse if you hadn't tried to help her. You're a remarkable woman, Mrs. L., and I'm proud of your generosity. And if you're ever in a financial squeeze, you let me know, okay?"

"You're a wonderful girl, Katy. I wish—" Mrs. L. broke off, evidently further embarrassed at whatever it was she wished, and Katy gave her a quick hug. If she couldn't have her own mother, Mrs. L. was surely the next best.

The phone was ringing just as Katy reached her bedroom. She picked it up eagerly.

"Hi, Katy."

Yes! "Hi, Jace." She knew she sounded eager and breathless and didn't care.

"I know it's late, but if I whine and groan will you take pity on me and invite me over for a cup of coffee?"

Katy laughed. "Save the whining and groaning for another occasion. You're invited. For coffee and cherry cobbler to go with it."

"You've been playing domestic goddess again?" he teased.

"More or less. Actually, I've kind of been at loose ends the last few days." She hesitated. "I've wondered if perhaps you were annoyed or angry with me."

"Because I haven't been over or called? Oh, Katy, no! Nothing like that." His response was gratifyingly quick and positive. "I've been gone all week. I'll explain when I come over, okay?"

"I'll unlock the front door, so just come on in when you get here."

Katy had barely unlocked the door and started a fresh pot of coffee when she heard the front door open. She couldn't run to meet him, but she knew she would have if she hadn't been encumbered with cast and crutches. She also knew her joy at seeing him was as obvious as any run when she let the crutches clatter to the floor and lifted her arms to encircle his neck.

He wrapped his arms around her in a big bear hug, and with a singing heart she knew he was as glad to see her as she was to see him.

"I've missed you, Katy," he said huskily against her hair, his breath warm on her ear.

She leaned back within the solid circle of his arms and studied each detail of his face as if it had been years rather than a few days. Gold flecks in his hazel eyes glowing with unconditional gladness to see her, warm smile, wonderfully imperfect little crook to his nose. But he also looked tired, she realized. She lifted a hand and smoothed the faint shadow of dark whiskers on his jaw with her fingertips.

"Are you telling me I need a shave before I can kiss you?" he teased.

In answer to that she raised on her tiptoes and kissed him, the kiss deepening as he responded with a rough sound in his throat. When he finally lifted his head, he grinned. "Maybe I'll have to go away more often if I get this kind of welcome home," he said huskily.

"Jace, where have you been? You didn't tell me you were going anywhere." She touched his jaw again, liking the roughness of masculine bristle against her fingertips.

He kissed her again, more lightly this time, and then slumped wearily onto the bench of the breakfast nook. "I didn't know I was going until the last minute. And then everything was so hectic down there."

"Down there?"

"San Francisco. I drove down Monday morning and just got back a couple of hours ago. You remember I told you I thought we were getting a corporate grant to buy new computers?"

She nodded.

"It all fell through. I went down to try to salvage the situation, but it didn't help."

"Oh, Jace, that's too bad. Why did they change their minds? Surely they could see what a worthy cause Damascus is!"

He tilted his head forward and massaged the back of his neck. "It wasn't anything to do with the school. Just number-crunching from the accounting department that showed profits were down. So this half-billion-dollar corporation decides it can't afford a few thousand to buy some underprivileged boys a

143

few computers after all." He lifted his head and smiled wryly. "I guess I'm whining after all, aren't I?"

"It seems to unfair!" She set a dish of cobbler in front of him and made a second trip with the coffee. She'd refined her crutch skills to the point where she could manage with just one for a few steps now, if she was careful.

"That's just the way things go. Anyway, I'm glad to be out of the city and back home. In spite of the song, I did *not* leave my heart in San Francisco."

A little hesitantly, Katy asked, "Jace, is the school having financial difficulties?"

"We're always short on money. It's our standard state of existence. But the Lord always provides and meets our needs one way or another." He smiled. "A big soup company just gave us a hundred cases of canned tomato sauce because the label was slightly off color. So be prepared for tomato everything the next time you eat with us. Tomato soup, tomato casserole, tomato cake, tomato pudding."

She smiled. "Tomato pudding sounds yummy. Am I invited for this Sunday?"

"Katy, you are *always* invited."

He dug into the cherry cobbler and moments later handed the empty dish back for seconds. "I feel better."

Katy found herself hoping there was truth in the old adage that the way to a man's heart was through his stomach. However, conscious that she'd been putting on a few pounds lately, not a wise move for a model, she ate only one small dish of cobbler herself. Then she had an idea.

"Maybe you've been approaching this computer situation from the wrong angle," she suggested thoughtfully.

Thirteen

Katy attended Sunday services in the chapel and stayed for the tomato-rich spaghetti dinner. Afterward, as Jace was driving her home, he casually asked if she had a Bible.

"I've never seen one around." Although she'd never looked.

"I'll bring you one. You might browse in Isaiah 49, or the thirteenth chapter of Hebrews. And the Psalms are always wonderful."

"You can bring it, but I'm not going to read it!"

He gave her a sideways glance. "Apparently you've read the Bible sometime, or you wouldn't know what you do about what's in it."

She couldn't argue with the fact that she did seem to have some unexplainable biblical understanding. "Knowledge isn't belief," she stated flatly.

Jace smiled. "God is working on you," he said with an annoyingly serene assurance. The next day, when he arrived to take her back to the river with the boys, he had a Bible for her. She tossed it into the living room, not watching to see where it landed. Jace exaggerated a cringe at her irreverent handling of his gift, but all he said was a cheerful, "God's Word has endured much worse and survived."

It was a fun afternoon, the hottest day yet. The boys splashed and paddled with noisy exuberance, sometimes deliberately dumping themselves in the water, and they joined together to toss Mac into the river to celebrate his birthday. With the cast enclosing her leg like an itchy trap and perspiration plastering her T-shirt to her back, Katy worked up sufficient courage to sit at the edge of the calm section of the river and cool one foot in the chilly water. The savage, churning white water on the far side of the river still distressed her, but she was okay if she kept her gaze close to her own feet.

Later in the week Jace reported that he'd acted on her suggestion and contacted a computer company about a direct donation of computers, and they sounded receptive to the idea. He said he might make a trip to Texas later to pitch the idea in person.

On Saturday, when Mrs. L. returned from Wilding with the mail, she handed Katy a letter with a New York postmark and unfamiliar handwriting. Katy opened it with the buzz of excitement always aroused by the possibility of some revelation that might jolt her memory out of hiding. Inside was a scrawled note reading, "We've never received reimbursement for the charges when we shipped all your stuff. $169.25. It's been months now. Please!!!" followed by the signature *Stephanie* swirling with look-at-me loops.

Katy showed the curt note to Mrs. L. "Is this one of my roommates?"

Mrs. L. slapped her own cheek with a stricken expression. "Oh, my! I must not have sent them the money to pay for shipping all your things out here. How could I have been so forgetful? I guess I just had so much on my mind."

"It's no big deal," Katy assured her. "I'll do it right away. In fact, I'll call her right now and tell her the money is on its way."

Mrs. L. looked in her address book but couldn't locate the phone number of the apartment where Katy had lived in New York, but Katy found it scribbled in the back of the phone book. She dialed the number from the kitchen phone, and a very young, chipper voice said, "Hi!"

"Stephanie?"

"No, this is Nikki. Stephanie's out."

Did she know Nikki? Cautiously Katy said, "Hi. This is Katy...Kat Cavanaugh."

"Oh, *hi*. You used to live here didn't you? I'm the new roommate. I just moved in with Steph and Linda a few weeks ago. Actually I've only been in New York a couple months. The agency may send me to Paris." Nikki giggled as she chattered, as if she were on the giddy adventure of a lifetime. "Oh, hey, hold on. Steph just came in."

An unintelligible exchange of words, and then a sultry voice spoke into the phone. "Hello, Kat."

The words sounded more like a claws-bared challenge than a greeting between old friends. Katy drew back, dismayed at the open flare of hostility, and she was suddenly reminded of what Barry had said about her former roommates' envy. She decided she was not going to be drawn into some unpleasant exchange.

"I just called to apologize for not sending the money earlier to reimburse you for shipping my things out. I'll put a check in the mail immediately."

"Oh. Well, thanks." Stephanie sounded as if this unexpected cooperation tipped her off balance.

"And I appreciate your going to all the trouble of doing the packing and shipping. Again, I'm sorry about the delay in getting the money to you. Things have been rather...unsettled here."

Brief silence, as if Stephanie was perhaps remembering the careless packing, which had resulted in the ruin of several expensive items. Katy had no intention of mentioning the damage, although she had to admit hoping Stephanie was feeling at least a few pinpricks of guilt.

"That's okay," Stephanie murmured. If there was any guilt, it obviously wasn't pricking very deeply. "We were all surprised when you wanted everything shipped out there. You hadn't said anything about not coming back when you left. How are you doing?" Now the voice held reluctant curiosity.

"Just fine."

"What do you *do* there? Isn't it terribly isolated?"

"It is rather isolated, but I like it. Mostly I've just been reading and thinking, doing some cooking."

"You, Kat, the one who said housework was for peons, stooping to *cooking?*"

"Actually, I go by the name of Katy now," Katy said, startled by both the reminder of her own snobbish attitude and the sneer in Stephanie's voice.

She half expected the other woman to make some derisive comment about the name adjustment, but instead Stephanie jumped to what she apparently considered a more important subject. "You don't have any intention of coming back to New York?"

"I'm not sure. Barry Alexander flew out a few days ago to talk to me...."

"Barry! Surely you're not thinking about going back to that loser!"

"Loser?"

"Oh, come on, Kat. He's putting up a big front, but everybody knows that agency is going under. Even you finally admitted you'd made a big mistake signing with him and that you should have dumped him long before you did. *I'd* have dumped him the minute he came up with that *pathetic* little engagement ring."

"I don't think I'd call three carats a 'pathetic little ring'!" Katy retorted, suddenly annoyed with Stephanie's superior scorn. She had a sudden sharp suspicion that the slipshod packing of her belongings may have been more deliberate than careless.

"Three carats?" Stephanie laughed gleefully. "C'mon, Katy,

get real! That diamond could barely make half a carat. If it even was a diamond."

This whole conversation was so petty, so astonishingly mean spirited, that Katy was disgusted. And ashamed that she'd risen to the bait of Stephanie's taunt about the ring. Barry was right about her roommates. No wonder she'd wanted out of that apartment. She started to hang up but paused, attention suddenly darting back to Stephanie's earlier statement.

"Are you saying I quit Barry's agency?" she asked cautiously.

"Quit? Kat, that scene you threw at his oh-so-ritzy cocktail party was a classic. Tearing up your contract with him, burying that ring in the shreds, soaking the whole mess in champagne, and wadding it into a ball and throwing it at him!" Briefly Stephanie sounded admiring, an admiration that appalled Katy, although not as much as hearing what *she* had done appalled her. Then Stephanie's tone turned mocking. "Yes, Kat, I'd say you definitely quit both Barry and his nickel-and-dime agency."

Katy tried to swallow her shock. "What did Barry do?"

"What could he do? You were the only model he's ever had who wasn't a complete *nobody*. He laughed and tried to pretend it was just a little lovers' spat."

"Were you there?" Katy challenged. "Or is this all just some rumor or gossip you heard?"

"No, I wasn't there," Stephanie admitted. "But I was here when he stormed in after the cocktail party, grabbed you around the throat, and threatened to kill you!"

"*Kill me?*"

"He thought the two of you were alone, I suppose, and he sure looked and sounded mad enough to do it. But he backed off when Connor and I came out of the bedroom and I ran for the phone to call the police. I guess he came to his senses then and decided the agency was in enough trouble without that kind of publicity."

Katy remembered the moment of fear she'd felt when Barry was here at the ranch and she'd thought he was going to strike her. Was he capable of actual violence?

"Why are you asking about all this?" Stephanie suddenly demanded suspiciously. "You were there. You know what happened. And you sound odd. What is this, Kat, one of your sly little I-just-can't-remember-anything-about-that games? Like the time you borrowed my Anne Klein dress without asking and somehow couldn't remember ruining it with that awful wine stain? Or the time you insisted you had no idea Linda was crazy about Dave Arnold or you'd never have gone out with him? Or how you could never quite remember when it was your turn to vacuum the apartment or take out the trash?"

Katy swallowed, knowing the incriminating list would probably go on and on if she let it. Apparently her roommates had accumulated plenty of ammunition to fuel their vindictive handling of her belongings. "Actually, I was in an accident."

Stephanie didn't wait for details or offer sympathy. Digging into memories of Katy's past misdeeds had apparently revved her anger, and it exploded in fury now. "Oh, were you?" she snapped. "An *accident.* How unfortunate. But it couldn't have happened to a more deserving person. Look, just send the money, okay? And then stay out of our lives!"

The phone slammed down. Katy numbly replaced the receiver at her end of the line.

Barry had lied to her. Katy did not really trust Stephanie, but her former roommate's description of events had the savage snarl of truth. But when Barry discovered Katy now had no memory of those past actions, he'd glibly decided to take advantage of her amnesia and pretend no split had ever occurred between them!

"Katy, sweetie, are you all right?" Mrs. L. touched Katy's arm anxiously. "Oh, dear, I know I shouldn't have been listening, but you started to get so pale!"

What had happened when Barry came to the ranch several months ago? That would have been after the break between them. Had he come to try to patch things up? Or carry out his threat? Had there been another ugly argument? And what had her response been?

Katy wobbled to the breakfast nook and gave Mrs. L. the details of the phone conversation. "Do you remember what happened when Barry was here? Were we arguing?"

Mrs. L. tilted her head thoughtfully. "Maybe things were a little tense. I remember you stomping away from the breakfast table one morning, and when I came in to get the dishes, he was wiping something off his face."

Probably, Katy thought in dismay, because she had thrown it there. "How long was he here?"

"Well, let's see. Two or three days, I think. But I really don't remember for certain, sweetie."

"Did he know I was planning to go away for a while?"

"I have no idea, hon."

Katy briefly wondered whether it would be possible to check through old records of the airlines and find out if Barry had actually flown back to New York immediately after leaving the ranch. Then she dismissed that entire line of thought as ridiculous. What was she speculating? That instead of flying back to New York, he'd stayed out here, intercepted her meeting in Redding, followed her, and three months later tossed her in the surf on the Oregon coast? Preposterous. He may have been furious with her for the personal and professional dumping she'd given him, but he had a modeling agency to run in New York, and stalking her for three months was crackpot stuff.

Yet he could have flown out from New York again later....

"You okay, sweetie?" Mrs. L. repeated anxiously.

Katy tried to smile. "Just my imagination working overtime. Maybe I need my afternoon nap."

The phone rang again, and she jumped nervously. Barry hadn't contacted her since leaving the ranch. Was he calling now? Or Stephanie calling back with further angry accusations? Mrs. L. squeezed Katy's arm and picked up the phone. She listened a moment and then held it out to Katy.

"Jace," she said with a reassuring smile, and Katy took the phone gladly.

Jace said he had to go look at a couple of calves a nearby rancher was willing to sell the school at a good price for their livestock project and would she like to come along?

Katy's first instinct was an instant *yes,* but, only half teasing, she asked, "Are you going to preach at me? Or give me a test on last Sunday's message?"

"I might. Or I might ask if you've been studying that Bible I gave you."

"I glanced at a few pages, but I didn't really study it." Actually, she'd read the complete book of Ruth, drawn to this inexplicably familiar-sounding narrative of how God faithfully guided and cared for a young widow in a strange land. But she'd slammed the book shut in anger when she reached the end. Maybe God worked that way for a few special favorites, but others he ruthlessly ignored or forgot.

"It'll grow on you," Jace said cheerfully.

"Don't count on it."

"Oh, but I am counting on it. Counting on you and God."

~ ~ ~ ~ ~

On the drive to the ranch she told Jace about calling her former roommate in New York and what Stephanie had told her about the scene at Barry's cocktail party. She sighed. "Every time I learn additional facts, the more disenchanted I am with myself."

Jace glanced sideways at her across the pickup seat. "Barry doesn't exactly win any gold stars, either," he pointed out. "He came out here and lied to you about everything."

"He could be worse than simply untrustworthy. Stephanie said that after the cocktail party, he came to the apartment and threatened to kill me." She hesitated. "And once, while he was here, I was a little afraid of him."

Jace braked so sharply that the seat belt jolted against Katy's chest. He pulled onto a wide spot on the shoulder of the road and turned to her. He didn't even ask what Barry had done to arouse her fear. He simply leaped full blast to her defense. "Katy, why didn't you tell me? If I thought you were in any danger, I'd have been over there before you could set the phone down!"

One glance at the dark anger in Jace's eyes told her he wouldn't be making polite conversation with Barry, and the harsh bite of his hands on the curve of her shoulders emphasized his raw strength to carry out the unspoken threat. A ridge of muscle ticked along the sharp edge of his jaw.

"Fisticuffs?" Katy teased shakily. "From a man of the Lord?"

He blinked, as if suddenly stepping back from the potent storm center of his emotions. His grip on her shoulders relaxed, and he massaged her upper arms lightly. He grinned ruefully. "The Lord and I do have to hold an occasional conference about my temper. It's nothing like it used to be, but an injustice or threat, especially to someone I care about, can still

153

push my buttons. Have you been in touch with Barry since he returned to New York?"

She momentarily lingered in the sweet music of *someone I care about* before answering his question. "No. But if he does call, I'm going to confront him with this."

Jace frowned. "Why don't you just let it go, Katy? Does it really matter now? He's there, you're here, and it's all in the past."

"Fine forgive-and-forget talk from a man who a moment ago sounded ready to tear the man apart piece by piece!"

"Sometimes my emotions and muscles have been known to fly into action before my brain gets into gear," Jace admitted. "But it's been a long time. And I just don't see any point in confronting him, Katy. It sounds as if the guy could be dangerous."

"But, as you pointed out, he's there and I'm here. And I think he should know that he can't put something over on me just because my memory is missing," she argued stubbornly.

"But if you aren't going back to modeling anyway—"

"I haven't decided that for certain."

"Perhaps it's just hopeful thinking on my part," he admitted.

"But what else could I do? Modeling is apparently all I know." This wasn't the first time she'd confronted that fact. She smiled wryly. "Not that, at the moment, I actually know anything about modeling, either."

"You could work at Damascus." He tilted his head thoughtfully. "I wonder what you could do there."

"I do seem to know a little about computers," she said. "I managed to find my way around on the one my mother used."

"Really?" He sounded surprised but accepted the information as if that settled everything. "Well, then, that's it. You can work in our office. The pay isn't great, but the boss is fantastic. Take a memo, Miss Cavanaugh. Remind the cook that not all one hundred cases of that tomato sauce have to be used up by the end of the month."

Katy laughed, and the mood lightened. He pulled back onto the gravel road. At the ranch, Katy stayed in the pickup, enjoying the scents of sun-warmed corral dust, sweaty horses, and fresh-cut hay lying in neatly raked rows in a nearby field, while Jace inspected the whiteface calves. A blacksmith was shoeing a horse by the corral fence, and she watched, fascinated, as he heated a metal shoe red hot and then plunged it into a bucket of cold water with a sizzle of steam. Jace and the rancher loaded the frisky calves into the back of the pickup, where they immediately made Katy laugh by poking their noses through the slats and smearing the rear window of the pickup. On the way home Jace sang a deliberately nasal version of *Git along little dogies,* repeating the line because that was apparently all he knew of the song, and Katy laughingly joined in. But when he dropped her off at the house, he turned serious again.

"Katy, promise you won't let Barry come out here again. Just tell him to buzz off, that you're not interested in him or his agency. I really think he could be dangerous."

"Oh, I don't think so. Back in New York he was probably just blowing off steam after I humiliated him at the cocktail party. And here, except for that one tiny moment, which I may have imagined anyway, he couldn't have been nicer."

"I'd still rather he stayed back in New York where he belongs."

"Jealous?" she teased hopefully.

"Maybe that's all it is," he granted. "But sometimes guys who make threats carry them out."

Fourteen

There were no threats or messages of any kind from Barry, and after a few uneasy days Katy relaxed. Apparently he'd decided pursuing either a personal or business relationship with her was a lost cause.

She attended Sunday services in the chapel two weeks in a row. The second time she heard a newly arrived boy whisper to another boy, "Who's that lady with the no-hair haircut?" and the answer was, "That's Mr. Foster's girlfriend." Jace didn't comment, just looked at her and grinned, and she didn't know whether to be insulted at the "no-hair haircut" description—she did have *some* hair now!—or joyful at being identified as "Mr. Foster's girlfriend."

Joyful, she decided recklessly. Because she was falling in love with him. No doubt about it. Love was in the air. And in her heart, soul, and bones!

Jace drove her into Yreka for the appointment to have the cast removed. After a final x-ray to be certain the leg had healed properly within the cast, the doctor got out a little saw and buzzed merrily through this stiff companion she was only too glad to be rid of. But when the cast fell away, and she stared at what was underneath, she didn't know whether to laugh or cry. This wasn't a *leg*. This was a pale, wimpy noodle, its long length interrupted only by a bony bump pretending to be a knee. Now she wished she'd worn long pants, but she hadn't, and she had to return to the waiting room with the leg fully on display in shorts.

Jace gallantly made no "pale noodle" comparisons, simply

gave her a reassuring kiss on the nose and took her to the best steakhouse in town to celebrate.

Back home, she tottered carefully to the bedroom to rest for a few minutes. Freedom from the cast felt wonderful, and she was already planning all the things she could do now, but at the moment she had to admit to being exhausted. She'd barely stretched out on the bed, however, when the phone rang. She waited for Mrs. L. to pick up, but after six rings Katy reached for the phone. "Hello."

"Hi, Kat."

She recognized his voice instantly. "Katy," she corrected sharply.

"You don't sound very glad to hear from me."

She sat up, swinging both legs to the floor. "Actually I am, Barry. I have something to discuss with you."

"Good. I'd have called sooner, but I wanted to give you space and time to work things out. But I remembered that today the cast was supposed to come off, and I wanted to find out if everything went okay."

In spite of her antagonism toward him, Katy was reluctantly impressed that he'd remembered this date and sounded so concerned.

"Everything's fine. The leg is still weak, of course. I lost a lot of muscle. But I'll be exercising and walking to strengthen it."

"Good," he repeated. "I hope what you wanted to talk to me about is when you're coming back to New York?"

"Not exactly." Bluntly she repeated everything Stephanie had told her. With no effort to be tactful she said flatly, "You lied to me, Barry. About both our personal and professional relationship."

If she thought he'd cower and grovel, cornered by the truth, she was mistaken.

"You're accepting Stephanie's word over mine, just like that?" Barry challenged. "Doesn't it occur to you that *she* could be lying?"

Katy returned a challenge of her own. "Stephanie doesn't know I have amnesia. How could she possibly think she could convince me things happened differently than they really did? As far as she knows, I know *exactly* what happened, because I was there."

Barry retreated fractionally. "I wouldn't say she's necessarily lying. But she wasn't at the cocktail party, and rumors and gossip have a way of expanding and changing shape."

True, Katy conceded. "But Stephanie was there, in the flesh, when you stormed into the apartment and threatened to kill me!"

She detected a moment of surprise when he realized she knew about that threat, but he hid it smoothly. "You have to remember, Katy, that Stephanie was furious with me because I wouldn't sign her with the agency. And you know the old saying about the fury of a woman scorned. She's been out to get me for a long time. And the last thing she wants is for you to return to New York, Katy. You're too much hot competition for her, and if she can alienate you from me, there's much less chance you will come back."

Yes, Stephanie was vindictive, Katy had to admit, remembering the state of her possessions in those cartons. Not that Katy herself would win any awards for sterling character, she also had to admit ruefully.

"Yes, I was upset when I came to the apartment," Barry continued. "That cocktail party was important to me. Influential people were there, and I was angry and hurt at what you said and did. But I knew you'd had too much to drink and weren't really responsible for your actions. And Stephanie has made her own overblown, overdramatized interpretation of what happened there at the apartment. I suppose I did mutter something about being mad enough to kill you. But it was nothing more than what a husband might grumble about his wife, 'If that woman interrupts my football game one more time, I'm gonna murder her.' Vicious sounding, if taken literally, but really quite meaningless."

Katy frowned and rubbed her palm across her pale thigh. "What about the ring?"

"It's true that at the cocktail party you rather flamboyantly returned the first ring I gave you. But you apologized and accepted another one, and it *was* three carats, Katy, if size matters to you." He sounded reproachful. "And that wasn't our contract you made such a melodramatic display of ripping to shreds at the party. It was several pages of instructions for my new VCR."

He laughed lightly, and Katy had to admit there was a certain humor in making high drama out of ripping up VCR instructions. If it was true, of course.

"Katy, you're not really afraid of me, are you, just because of that meaningless threat?"

She swallowed. "I'm not sure."

"Don't be. Because I love you, Katy. And I'm not giving up on *us.*"

His voice was low and fierce with determined passion, and confusion tinged with guilt rolled through her. Had she too readily accepted Stephanie's virulent accusations?

"Are you afraid, Katy?"

She noted the rephrasing of the question, now asking not if she were afraid of him but simply if she were afraid. She hesitated, then reluctantly admitted, "Sometimes."

"Of what? Tell me, Katy. I want to know."

"I don't know. Sometimes I just feel uneasy. Apprehensive. As if...things may not be quite what they appear to be. Without a memory I feel so vulnerable."

"Be careful, Katy," he said suddenly, with an odd urgency. "Don't be too trusting of anybody. That old housekeeper who got the big bucks in the will and that boyfriend of hers who's always skulking around—who knows what they're up to? And that son of hers, what's his name? The pint-sized Dry-Cleaning King that she thinks is so wonderful he could walk on water, which isn't half as wonderful as *he* thinks he is."

Katy cut into the tirade with a surprised question. "You know Evan?"

"Yeah, I met him when I flew out to talk to you about the big cosmetics company deal just before you took off to catch amnesia."

"You don't *catch* amnesia." This whole conversation was turning ridiculous, but Barry wasn't through yet.

"Then there's that whole gang of teenage delinquents from across the road. I'll bet a raid of that place would turn up enough knives and weapons made out of pitchfork tines or something to fill a truck. And most of all, watch out for that religious nut you had the big blowup with about the land deal."

"Barry, those are good kids at Damascus! And if you think flinging accusations against my friends is going to make me feel any more loving toward *you*—"

"I'm not accusing. I'm just saying be on guard. Who knows what any of them are up to? The religious nut would like nothing better than—"

Katy had had enough. "Barry, you are out of your mind!" She angrily slammed down the phone without saying goodbye. She was not going to listen to this! At this point she wasn't certain who was lying to her, Stephanie or Barry, about what had happened in New York. But she was not going to let Barry make ugly accusations about her friends and the man she loved!

Fifteen

Katy determinedly practiced the strengthening exercises the doctor had recommended and gradually lengthened her daily walks. Jace often joined her in the evening, usually scolding protectively that she was trying to do too much too soon.

But there was so much she wanted to do! She'd been imprisoned in the cast for most of her remembered life, and she wanted to do everything she'd missed. Walk and run, drive and climb!

The pale leg tanned in the summer sun, filled out, and strengthened. She climbed the stairs to her mother's studio, cautiously walking upright on two legs rather than scooting on her bottom. She flexed her skills on the computer, worked in the garden, took the convertible out for short spins. She talked to Mrs. L.'s son again, beginning to believe that if anyone could jog her memory, it was probably Evan. A couple of times they spent over an hour companionably talking about their childhood together. Nothing broke through, but several times she felt an almost-glimmer of familiarity, and she urged him to come visit anytime.

During one of those conversations, she started to say goodbye, then remembered she wanted to ask him about meeting Barry. Evan hemmed and hawed on the subject of her ex-fiancé, which was what Katy considered Barry now, dodging direct comment by saying he'd been busy helping his mother around the ranch and really hadn't gotten to know Barry.

Finally Katy realized what was going on. She laughed.

"Okay, I get the picture. You're using that old guideline 'If you can't say something nice about someone, don't say anything at all.'"

Evan's answering laugh sounded guilty. "Could be, I guess. I don't like to run people down. Actually, I suppose he was okay, maybe a little, well, New Yorkish for a Texan like me. But the two of you were fighting about something, and I kept wanting to jump in and protect you, but Mom said don't play Lone Ranger out to rescue the helpless maiden, that it was none of my business."

Katy laughed again. From those photos she'd seen of Evan, she could indeed imagine him galloping in for the rescue. Then she asked a serious question. "By fighting, do you mean anything physical?"

"As far as I know, it was just words, although sometimes he sounded angry enough to add something physical. I was concerned, but I had to leave before he did, and I guess it turned out okay. Mom said you got so disgusted with him that finally you just kicked him out."

Another small point Barry hadn't bothered to mention, Katy thought wryly. "Do you remember my saying anything to you about leaving the ranch and going off somewhere with a friend or friends?"

"You did mention something once about just getting away for a while to make some decisions about your career and life, but you weren't specific about it. I had the impression that actually *doing* it was an impulsive decision you made after I'd left the ranch."

She knew there were still decisions she must make about her modeling career and, if she wanted to return to it, how. From what she could determine so far, she hadn't exactly left a red carpet of good will in New York. She also knew she couldn't wait indefinitely for the dark pit in her mind to open. She might simply have to acknowledge that it wasn't going to happen and get on with her life. Yet every night when the insects sang their summer song in the meadow, the word *crickets* came back to haunt her and raise questions. She knew her procrastination was also connected to an uncertainty about how Jace felt about her. He was fond of her and strongly attracted to her, she was certain, but were his feelings moving toward the love already blossoming within her?

She drove herself into Yreka for her scheduled checkup on the leg, and she passed that final exam with flying colors. On the same day she went to a beauty shop Mrs. L. recommended. The hairdresser still hadn't much to work with, but she managed to coax a bit of shape and curl into Katy's spiky blond bristles, and Jace approvingly complimented the results that evening.

Two days later the school threw a big Fourth-of-July celebration, and people came from all over for the barbecue and games and fireworks. The afternoon sun blazed white hot in a cloudless blue sky, just what a Fourth of July should be, Katy thought, happy and exhilarated as she and Mrs. L. walked across the road to join the milling crowd. Cars and pickups already filled the pasture beside the barn.

Katy wandered the grounds in her pink shorts, T-shirt, and flowered hat, curious about everything, glad a tiny wisp of curl showed from under the hat now. The sound system blared music, everything from lively gospel to country and western, with Mac's rich voice interrupting occasionally to announce games or give their results. Horses whinnied from the corral, enthusiastic yells cheered the competitors in the games, and kids playing tag dodged through the crowd like small, erratic missiles. Over it all hung a warm haze of summer dust and fun and the fragrant, smoky scent of barbecuing chicken.

She saw Joe herding kids through the small petting zoo of calves, lambs, chickens, and ducks, found Shirley and Alice dispensing lemonade and soft drinks, spotted Mac speaking from a stand built over the games area. But where was Jace?

Then she heard another sound. Thunks. Splashes. Shrieks. She followed the sound and there he was, just climbing out of the water, wet jeans clinging to long legs, glistening rivulets of water running down bare chest and off the wet hair hanging in his eyes. He climbed back to a perch above the dunk tank and crossed his arms in challenge. "Okay, you sharpshooters!"

Thunk!

The ball hit to the left of the target. "I knew you couldn't hit the broad side of a barn, Jerry," Jace jeered cheerfully.

Thunk! The ball slammed the metal target dead center, Jace plunged into the dunk tank with a tidal splash that rolled water over the sides, and the boy named Jerry jumped up and down gleefully.

"Sheer dumb luck," Jace called with exaggerated exasperation as he climbed from the tank. And promptly went down again as another boy clobbered the target with the ball.

Suddenly Jace spotted Katy in the crowd. "Hey, let the lady through!" he called. "I need some rest up here!"

The boys made way for Katy, but she shook her head. Someone thrust a ball into her hand. Then someone shoved her, and there she was, up front on the firing line. Reluctantly she tossed the first ball. It slopped ignominiously into the tank, far from the target.

"See, what'd I tell you? Now I'm as safe as a baby in a cradle!" Jace swayed his arms in teasing imitation of rocking a baby.

Oh, yeah? Katy threw another ball. She missed the target, but the ball clunked solidly on the backstop. She paused, concentrating. A faintly-remembered *something* came over her. She hauled her arm back, gazed narrow-eyed at the target, and down he came!

The crowd cheered. Katy waited until Jace was back on the perch, then dusted her hands with a smug air of success. But before she turned away, she grinned and recklessly blew him a kiss.

A few minutes later Mac's voice calling everyone to eat came over the loudspeaker, and he offered a prayer of blessing and thanks. Boys from the school lined up behind a long table decorated in red, white, and blue to serve the food. Little Ramsey grinned at Katy and handpicked a special piece of American-flag cake with a star on it for her. She and Mrs. L. found empty places at a picnic table and dove into what Katy instinctively thought of as perfect Fourth-of-July food: barbecued chicken, potato salad, baked beans, and coleslaw.

She was just finishing her second piece of chicken when Jace plopped down beside her with a full plate of his own, and Joe joined Mrs. L. on the opposite side of the picnic table.

"Traitor," Jace muttered. "Who'd have thought you could hit the target like that? Those boys dunked me so many times I could have passed for a prune, and then you came along and did it too."

He'd donned a denim shirt, and it hung open over his hard-muscled chest. His dark hair fell with boyish abandon across his face. He looked rugged and carefree and teasingly handsome, not a prune wrinkle in sight.

Later, as the summer dusk deepened, Jace brought a blanket to spread on the grass. Joe, who seemed to know a little about everything, disappeared around the barn to set off the fireworks. The first rocket exploded in a blaze of fiery red shot with twinkles of silver, and a fantastic display of color and light followed. Glittering skyfalls of rainbow colors, explosions shooting out of explosions so one sunburst became three, galaxy swirls of sparkling silver, shooting stars of gold, sky fountains of flaming color. Booming and squealing and whistling rockets, then echoes of appreciative oohs and aahs from the crowd. Katy sat with her back against Jace's chest, secure within the curve of his arms, excited but dreamy. And never happier.

A stationary display of the Stars and Stripes ignited in a final blaze of glory, and everyone stood as the grand strains of the national anthem poured from the sound system.

Immediately afterward the crowd stirred toward departure, companionable groups breaking up, saying good-byes, people calling to Jace that it was the best celebration ever. A general drift toward the parking area began as people hurried to beat the rush of traffic.

But Katy didn't move. She just stood there, muscles frozen. A blinding afterglow lingered in her eyes, a blaze of incandescent color and light that dizzied and dazzled her. But that wasn't what held her rigid, eyes wide open but unseeing. It was the shadows.

Shadows playing across a landscape of light somewhere inside her head. Dark figures, two of them. No, three! One smaller than the other two, three figures moving gently, almost in slow motion. She closed her eyes, straining to focus on the dark silhouettes hovering somewhere between her eyelids and that bottomless pit in her mind. *Come out where I can see you!* she commanded them fiercely. Then, pleadingly, *Please!* One figure turned a featureless face to her, as if it were about to speak.

"Katy! Katy! Are you all right?"

Katy blinked and looked up into Jace's concerned face. She shook her head trying dazedly to clear both eyes and mind, as if for a few moments she had wandered somewhere outside this earthly dimension. "I guess the fireworks just blinded me for a moment."

An acrid scent of burned-out fireworks hung in the air. Headlights streamed out of the parking area, and red taillights flickered on the road. The shadows within her head were gone now, the dark pit closed again. But they were the beginning of a memory, Katy thought fiercely. For the first time, she'd had the real beginning of a memory!

Mrs. L. touched her arm. "Katy?" She also sounded worried.

"You tried to do too much today," Jace said sternly. "Sit down again. We'll wait for the traffic to clear out. What happened?"

She obediently sank back to the blanket, but she didn't want to talk about this just yet, as if talking might destroy this tenuous connection with the past. She closed her eyes again, desperately willing the shadows to return, and Jace's arm tightened around her as if he knew she was struggling with something.

The traffic had thinned by the time Joe came out from behind the barn. Road dust hung heavy in the air. Katy stumbled to her feet.

"I'm okay. Mrs. L. and I can make it home alone."

"No way," Jace said with don't-argue-with-me finality. He wrapped his arm around Katy's shoulders, and Joe fell into step with Mrs. L. behind them.

At the house, Katy would have preferred to retreat to her room immediately, but Mrs. L. asked the men in for coffee. Jace and Joe sat at the breakfast nook rehashing the celebration, and Katy cut pie while Mrs. L. poured the coffee. At the table she didn't join the conversation, and finally Jace commented.

"Are you sure you're all right, Katy? You seem so quiet."

She swallowed. "After the flag display blazed, my eyes felt strange, and then something happened."

"Happened?" They all eyed her alertly.

"I saw these...shadows." Katy covered her eyes with her hands, desperately trying to re-create the moment. "Shadows of people, three people, inside my head. They were just silhouettes, so I couldn't tell who they were, but I know, *I know*, they were a memory trying to break through."

Katy pulled her hands away from her eyes and looked around at the three silent faces staring at her. No questions, no encouragement, nothing! Just those wide-eyed stares.

Katy managed a shaky laugh. "Why are you all looking at me as if I'd just sprouted another head?" She suddenly slapped her palm against the table, almost angry. "Don't you *want* me to remember?"

Another stretched-out moment of silence, with Jace and Joe and Mrs. L. poised like a trio of divers before a deadly plunge down a cliff, until finally Jace hunched forward and curled his hand around hers.

"Of course we want you to remember, Katy. It's just that—" He hesitated as if embarrassed about his true feelings. His glance flicked to the two faces now focused on him. "I don't know about anyone else, but I guess I'm afraid that if your memory comes back, you'll turn into the old Kat. And I've become rather fond of the new one."

Katy touched her throat. Would that happen? Would she become the old self-centered, greedy, vindictive Kat again? She glanced at Mrs. L., who shook her head a little helplessly.

"I'm sorry, Katy. I do want you to remember! It's terrible not to know your own past. And yet, since the accident, you've been so much more like the sweet little girl you used to be and less like the sophisticated, ambitious woman you became." She, too, sounded embarrassed and guilty for feeling that way. "But you know how hard I've tried to help you remember!"

"Yes, I know." Katy again tried to smile. "I guess if it comes to a vote, the old Kat just doesn't get re-elected to office."

Mrs. L. patted Katy's hand. "We just want what's best for you, sweetie. I think I know what you're remembering. It was a Fourth-of-July celebration your folks took you to when you were just a little girl. I wasn't there because I'd gone to visit a relative, but later you went on and on about the flag that burst into explosion and fire. So seeing something similar tonight must have triggered your memory."

Katy squeezed her eyes shut again. "But there were *three* figures, and one was smaller."

Mrs. L. beamed. "Yes, that's exactly right! And the third one was my Evan. Your folks offered to keep him over the holiday, and you all went to that Fourth-of-July celebration!"

Jace looked at his watch. "I'd better get back to the dorm. My turn to do bed check tonight. Walk me to the door, Katy?"

At the door, Katy stepped outside with him, where the star-filled night glowed with an endless glory that the temporary brilliance of exploding fireworks could never match. Jace put his arms around her.

"Maybe what I'm really afraid of is that if your memory returns, you'll also remember that you're in love with Barry."

"I don't think so." But she didn't *know* so, and she searched his dark eyes helplessly. Now she felt poised on the brink of plunging down that cliff herself. Would everything change if her memory returned?

His mouth dipped to hers, the kiss almost fierce, as if he desperately wanted to blot out any intruding memories that might come between them. Then the kiss turned gentler, sweeter, and when he lifted his mouth he still held her close. "Don't change, Katy," he whispered. "Please don't change."

⌃ ⌃ ⌃ ⌃ ⌃

On Saturday Jace left on his trip to Texas to persuade the computer company to donate the new equipment the school needed. He took Ramsey and another boy along as living examples of the work Damascus was doing.

Katy knew Jace would disapprove, but she didn't go to Sunday services in the chapel that week. Instead she packed a sandwich, an orange, and a bottle of flavored tea in a backpack she found in the garage. Today she was going to take an actual hike, and she had a special destination in mind. She scribbled a note to Mrs. L, who was sewing in her room, guiltily dodging explaining her plans in person because she knew the housekeeper would disapprove and fuss at her.

Jitters ruffled her nerves as she started across the meadow of waving grass behind the house. She determinedly soothed them. Jace never allowed the boys in this dangerous downstream area of white-water rapids, but there was no real danger to her. The river was not, after all, going to lash out and snatch her like some hungry animal.

And she had to try this. Last night, in that floating twilight between awake and sleep, the shadows had returned. Three shadows, sharp in dark silhouette but mysteriously featureless. Tantalizingly they flickered across the background of her mind, the small one sometimes blithely twirling and dancing. Within her mind she chased them, desperately calling to them. They seemed unaware of her existence, but they melted into the dark pit if she got too close. And somehow, no matter what Mrs. L. said, she wasn't convinced they were Thornton and Mavis and Evan.

Lying sleepless long after the shadows disappeared, she had worked out this plan. Her past had vanished in the wild surf of an Oregon beach. Making herself confront a similar wild-water danger here might be a way to jolt that past to life again, to change those flickering shadows into real faces.

She resolutely forced herself to ignore her apprehension and concentrate on the glorious summer day. Lush scents of meadow grass and blooming wildflowers, the tickle of grass on her bare legs, the soft call of an unseen quail. A yellow-and-black butterfly danced to silent music; a hawk circled effortlessly on an updraft of summer air; an iridescent hummingbird hovered over a flower. All so gloriously, serenely beautiful. The cats followed for a while, but they didn't like the tall grass. Eventually they sat down, meowing in melodramatic protest as she continued on. Laughing, she turned and shooed them homeward.

A few minutes later she stopped short when she stepped onto a harder, firmer-footed area of the meadow. What was this? Here, in a broad line arrowing in both directions, the grass grew only sparsely, as if at one time the ground had been scraped clean. At one end, something on the ground fluttered gently in the breeze, and near the flutter sunlight glinted on something metallic.

Puzzled, she walked in that direction, then stopped short again as understanding claw-clutched her stomach.

In theory she'd known this was out here, but this wasn't theory; this was agonizingly *real*. This was the crude airstrip where her father's plane had failed on takeoff. The thing gently billowing and fluttering was an old windsock, the pole to which it was attached fallen to the ground. This was where panic and terror had overtaken her parents, where they had plunged back to earth and died. And that metallic strip...

She whirled, heart pounding, feet poised to race for the haven of the house. Death suddenly felt so near, a cold fingertip on her spine, an eerie whisper in her ear.

She grabbed the straps of the knapsack to steady herself

and forced her feet to rivet to the ground. Yes, she was upset, she acknowledged, grabbing a deep breath to fight a disorienting dizziness. Coming without warning upon the scene of her parents' death, even seeing a scrap of their crashed plane, was a shocker. But she would not abandon her plan.

She rested a minute and then, ignoring the wobble in her legs, stepped off the blurred edge of the abandoned runway and strode purposefully toward the river.

Only a narrow strip of trees bordered the river here, where the meadow came almost to a point, with angled lines of deep forest on either side. But the growth was brushy and thick, and Katy ducked and squirmed to get through it, wishing she'd worn something that offered more protection than shorts. A blackberry bramble ripped her hand, and she paused to catch her breath and suck on the painful scratch. She couldn't see the river clearly, but a flicker of silvery white water gleamed through the thick branches, and the roaring water seemed to vibrate the very earth beneath her feet.

Katy forced herself to plunge ahead. She was closer to the water than she'd thought, she realized a moment later when the ground disappeared in a dropoff no more than a footstep ahead. She stopped short, then edged forward, holding a branch for support. Without warning the dirt crumbled beneath her. She screamed, and the rough branch burned her hand as her feet plunged into the hole. More dirt gave way as she frantically back-scrabbled to safety. Holding the branch with both hands, she peered downward, her gaze riveted to the dark water swirling ominously beneath the tangle of roots undercut by the rushing current.

Don't panic, she commanded herself fiercely. *Everything's okay.* This was what she had come for, to rattle her subconscious into giving up its secrets. Determinedly she lifted her gaze to the river.

The untamed beauty took her breath away. Roaring white water surged around boulders as large as cars, crashed with raw fury into dark, sharp rocks, avalanched over a plateau of bedrock. Slick hollows of green water swooped over hidden ambushes, then erupted into the savage froth of standing waves endlessly battling to climb upriver. Whirlpools and upsurges appeared and disappeared as if some deadly game played beneath the surface. Here the river's fury bleached the deep color of the water in the calm area upstream to a pale tinge of green beneath the turbulent white water. A rainbow quivered over one falling spray, delicately lovely against the raging chaos below, and misty droplets drifted and clung to Katy's face. And beneath the roar of river came the ominous gurgle of water flowing beneath the undercut bank.

She clutched the branch more tightly. Yes, oh so beautiful. But also treacherous and violent and savage, not just a rapids but a seething, boiling trap of death. She remembered Jace saying he'd foolishly taken a kayak through here once, but he'd never do it again.

Something large and dark churning in the water caught her gaze. A log, swept down from somewhere upstream, whirling and plunging through the rocks like some terrified creature. Momentarily it caught on a rock, quivering as water pressure battered it from both ends. Then one side won and flipped the log on end, as if it were no more than a stick of kindling. Katy suddenly felt the chill spike of personal threat, as if the river were demonstrating what it could do to her. Then, in a final warning, a swirling whirlpool sucked the log under, swallowing it whole. And it didn't come up again.

Okay, so the river could swallow a log, she granted, resolutely battling a raw panic threatening to engulf her. But it couldn't get her! She was safe here.

Then, like some unseen monster opening its mouth under

her and slyly mocking her claim of safety, the earth gave way beneath her feet again. The branch snapped when her full weight hit it. Legs sliding into dissolving earth, treacherous suck of dark water only inches below.

Frantically she clawed at anything she could reach—brush, brambles, rocks. She scrabbled upward, the exposed roots snagging her feet and legs like live tentacles. She screamed and kicked, never minding the rip and tear of skin and flesh. She was on her belly now, then scrambling, fighting to her feet, stumbling, running, tearing blindly through the brush, caring about nothing except getting away from the water. Because she'd been wrong! It *could* snatch and grab her!

Her wild flight didn't end until minutes later when her injured leg gave way and sent her sprawling on the ground. She simply lay there, painful stitch in her side, too weak to run or struggle further.

Lord, please!

No, she would not call on the Lord, she vowed fiercely. He didn't care!

Finally, when the sharp stitch dulled to a soreness beneath her ribs, she slowly sat up. Then she was confused. Where was she? If she'd been thinking straight, she'd have run toward the open meadow, but she hadn't done that. Instead, already upset by the shock of her parents' death scene, then panicked by the hungry clutch of the river, she'd blindly plunged deep into the forest. Now the sky was only a jigsaw puzzle of blue among tangled branches overhead, and the ground oozed an unpleasant scent of dampness and decay, as if the sun never reached here. She wrinkled her nose and wiped her hands on her shorts to rid them of the dark, gooey mud all around her.

She started to stand, but a glitter of something caught on a nearby bush stopped her. On her knees she cautiously picked the thing out of the stickery bush.

She stretched it between her hands, astonished. It was a gold chain, broken, with a heavy, astrological-design medallion hanging from it. How had it ever gotten way out here? And who did it belong to?

Bracing herself on the trunk of the nearby tree, she struggled to her feet. She still felt weak but no longer panicky. Her terrified flight even seemed melodramatic and foolish now. She took a moment to look within her mind. Were the shadows there, awakened to reveal faces and identities, as she had hoped? No. Nothing.

What she was, she realized wryly, was muddy, scratched, sore, and *lost*. She couldn't even hear the roar of the rapids here. She might, in fact, be off her own unfenced eighty acres. She eyed the sky again, but she couldn't tell exactly where the sun was through the ragged canopy of branches. And she was no backwoods survivalist capable of finding her way by sun directions anyway.

Knowing she wasn't going to become *un*-lost simply by standing there, she stuffed the necklace in her pocket and started walking. Within a few feet she had to wonder how she'd managed to get where she was. Now she had to detour trees and impassable clumps of brush and fight her way across rough ravines. Her backpack caught on vines and brambles, and she'd long since lost her hat. The thought finally occurred to her that even though she was lost, she had food, and she slumped against a supporting tree trunk and hastily downed sandwich, orange, and bottled tea. Then she started out again, hopefully heading toward what she thought was the sound of a vehicle on the road, only, a few minutes later, to find herself staring at a scrap of orange peel on the ground. She was simply going in circles!

She wandered for a good forty-five minutes more before stumbling out of the trees. She blinked in the bright sunlight of the open meadow. And there, only a few hundred yards away, stood the house! With Mrs. L. showing the ever patient Joe exactly how she wanted the wire cages placed over her tomato plants.

Katy refrained from doing what she wanted to do, which was run and hug them as if she'd been lost in the woods for a week! Instead, she casually sauntered up to them.

Mrs. L. took one look at her and gasped, "Katy, what on earth? Just look at you, child! Oh, I knew when I read your note that something terrible was going to happen."

She herded Katy inside like some misbehaving five-year-old, scolding all the time she was washing and disinfecting and applying ointment and Band-Aids. When they emerged from the bathroom, Mrs. L. still fussing, Joe was helping himself to a glass of lemonade from the refrigerator. He offered Katy one, and she accepted gratefully.

"Oh, I found something." Katy pulled the chain and gold medallion from the pocket of her shorts. She spread it on the kitchen counter.

"Where did you get that?" Mrs. L. gasped.

"I found it out in the woods."

"Where?"

"Actually, I don't know. I got all turned around and don't really know where I was."

"Katy, you mustn't go wandering off alone!" Mrs. L. scolded with surprising vehemence. "You could fall in the river or get lost in the mountains. And there's bear and maybe even cougars out there!"

Joe poked at the necklace with a bony finger. "Isn't that one you used to wear, Katy? For good luck or something?" He was, in his own quiet, reserved way, fairly friendly with her now. "Looks expensive, like real gold."

"Joe Barnes, you wouldn't know real gold from a real carrot," Mrs. L. declared. She sounded mildly exasperated. She draped the necklace across her hand, studied it critically, then dismissed it with a careless toss on the counter. "I certainly don't remember it, and I'm sure I would if Katy'd ever worn it. In the summer we sometimes get outside people sneaking across the property trying to find a way to the river. Probably one of them lost it."

Joe frowned, momentarily looking as if he'd like to argue, but he meekly backed down when Mrs. L. snatched the lemonade pitcher and told him it was time to get back to the tomatoes. "And just look at those muddy shoes!" she exclaimed as she shooed Joe toward the door.

Katy had removed her dirty shoes when she entered the house. Mrs. L. now picked them up and, holding them at arm's length, marched into the laundry room. "I declare, sometimes…"

Whatever Mrs. L. declared faded behind the closed door and a rush of water into the metal sink. Joe went back to the tomatoes, and Katy took the necklace to her bedroom and dropped it on the table by her bed. The necklace did look expensive, but the gold medallion was too heavy and ornate for her taste, and she didn't care for the astrological design.

She was suddenly exhausted, worn out both physically and emotionally by the day's events. She'd probably have been better off, she thought wryly, if she'd simply gone to Sunday services. She undressed, wrinkling her nose in distaste at the smears of dark mud on her shorts. She rinsed them off in the sink and showered, in the process also washing off most of the ointment Mrs. L. had so carefully applied.

She fell asleep and woke groggily to the ringing of the phone. Then she came awake with alacrity. Jace? "Hello," she said eagerly.

"Hi, Katy."

Not Jace. "Hello, Barry." She didn't try to conceal her lack of enthusiasm.

"I've been thinking about you a lot, Katy. Do I dare hope you've been thinking about me too?"

"Oh, yes, I've been thinking about you." But not with the absence-makes-the-heart-grow-fonder longing for which he was probably hoping.

"Is the leg getting stronger?"

"Yes. I took a long walk today." She didn't go into details.

"Are you also doing the exercises the doctor recommended?" His tone was solicitous.

"Yes." With no encouragement on that subject, he tried a different one.

"This must be a beautiful time of year there in the mountains."

"Yes, very nice." A little guiltily she realized he was trying hard to be friendly and pleasant, and she was being quite rude. Which was characteristic enough for the old Kat, of course, but Katy felt uncomfortable with it now even though her feelings toward Barry were hostile and suspicious. So when he asked if her memory was showing any signs of progress, she answered more fully than she might have if he'd asked the question first.

"No real progress, although a few times I've had these kind of odd shadows flitting around in my head. Mrs. L. thinks they're a memory of a Fourth-of-July celebration I went to a long time ago with my parents and her son, Evan."

"Is that what *you* think?"

"I'm not sure. Maybe." She was lying with one arm under her on the bed, and when she shifted to a more comfortable position, the phone cord almost brushed the necklace off the small table. Impulsively she asked, "Barry, do you remember my ever wearing a medallion with an astrological design on a gold chain?"

"No, I don't think so. Why do you ask?" The question held an odd wariness.

"Because I found it—" She broke off. Dark smears of mud on her shorts. Heavy dark mud clinging to her shoes. She'd seen that gooey mud before.

On Barry's shoes.

Sixteen

arry went on talking about gold hoop earrings he'd once given her, but Katy's mind lingered on *mud*. Carrying the phone, she stretched the long cord until she could peer into the bathroom sink. A faint dark line still stained the shorts, but she'd effectively washed away the dried mud itself. And Mrs. L. had washed it off the shoes.

She dismissed a small rush of disappointment. What did she think, that a similarity in mud was somehow going to incriminate Barry? And even if it was exactly the same mud, so what? Barry could accidentally have wandered into it when he got turned around in the woods, just as she had. And in what ominous activity did she think *mud* would incriminate Barry?

This whole line of thought was so melodramatic and over-wrought that she had to wonder if she wasn't being totally unfair to Barry.

"…consider coming back to New York now?" he was saying. "I'd feel so much better if you were here. And being in familiar surroundings here might be more help in restoring your memory than the ranch," he added persuasively.

That thought had never occurred to Katy, but it was true. She had spent far more time in New York than she ever had on the ranch. Should she make plans to return to New York?

Jace returned in the middle of the week, pleased with the results of his trip.

"They're giving us twenty computers!" he said exultantly. "Twenty! They're not the very latest model, only 120 MHz and 1.2 GB hard drive, and the newest ones are faster and bigger than that, of course. But they're a big improvement over those old 386s the boys have been using."

Those numbers didn't make complete sense to Katy, but, surprisingly, there was a vague familiarity to them. Why? Crickets and computers, she thought, shaking her head. A strange combination indeed. Plus the nagging feeling that never quite went away, that there was something desperately important she must do that she'd forgotten.

Jace went on talking about the trip to Texas, gestures occasionally punctuating his enthusiasm. They were walking along the shoulder of the gravel road. Jace had suggested hiking the rutted lane back to the river, but Katy had shuddered and declined. Her aversion to water deeper than a bathtub or more forceful than a shower was stronger than ever.

A faint scent of dust lingered in the air from the log-truck traffic of the day, and a whiff of fresh hay drifted from the school's barn. The snow line had crept up on Mt. Shasta now, but summer sunshine couldn't penetrate the summit depths, and the peak retained its snowy splendor. Katy had brought along the gold chain and now brought it out to show Jace. She didn't explain how or where she'd acquired it, not wanting to influence his first reaction.

"Have you ever seen this before?"

"Looks like one you used to wear. You were into some New Age-y and astrological stuff. You also had a crystal you wore sometimes. Does it feel familiar in some way?" He grinned a little guiltily. "I've been reading whatever I can get my hands on about amnesia. I think a lot of it is psychobabble, and some of it is simply far out and preposterous, about reincarnation and multiple personalities. But there seemed a sensible logic in one piece I read that said certain personal objects might trigger a memory."

Katy swallowed, not quite knowing how to broach this subject. "Jace, sometimes I wonder if I can't arouse any memories of the ranch, or you, or Barry, or this necklace because they don't exist."

Jace stopped and tilted his head as he turned to face her. The setting sun touched his dark hair with a hint of auburn fire and brought out the gold flecks and green depths in his hazel eyes. "I'm not following you."

"Jace, what if Mrs. L. made a mistake when she identified me? What if I'm *not* Katy Cavanaugh? What if I'm someone else entirely?"

For a moment she thought he might laugh and tease her about her weird imagination, but he didn't. He put his arms on her shoulders and studied her eyes and nose and mouth. He stepped back to examine her body with an intensity that would have embarrassed her if it were not so clinical.

He smiled. "You sure look like Katy Cavanaugh to me."

"But I'm not like *Kat* Cavanaugh. You and everyone else admit that."

"Your doctor said personality changes were a possible by-product of amnesia. I've read that, too."

"I know. And maybe all these strange thoughts I'm having are simply frustration that the shadows in my head won't come into the open and be recognizable. And then finding the necklace way out there in the woods."

"In the woods?" Jace seemed startled. He looked more closely at the medallion swinging from her fingers. "I thought you just ran across it in a jewelry box or drawer."

"No."

"Where in the woods?"

She explained about the shock of the airstrip, the ground

185

crumbling beneath her at the river, and running until she was lost. She shivered as the panic echoed through her, and he wrapped her in the security and comfort of his arms.

"C'mon, let's go back to the house. You're upset."

She lifted her head and tried to smile. "And advancing from run-of-the-mill amnesiac to weirdo with delusions?"

He kissed her on the nose. "We're all a little weird sometimes."

He tucked her arm under his, but she resisted his tug toward home. "Let's keep walking. At the risk of sounding even stranger, I have another theoretical question to ask."

"Ask away."

"Suppose, just for the sake of supposing, that I really am not Katy Cavanaugh. Suppose I'm really someone else entirely. Jane Doe from Denver, perhaps. Or Judy Jones from Juneau."

He closed his eyes and pretended to be in deep concentration. "Okay, I'm supposing. You're really Judy Jones from Juneau. Shouldn't some other Joneses be looking for you?"

"Yes, but that's a separate issue. Right now let's stick with this one. Let's just say Mrs. L. made a mistake in identifying me and I'm not Kat Cavanaugh."

"Okay. Big mistake."

She had a feeling he was simply humoring her, but she barged on. "Then what happened to the real Kat Cavanaugh?"

Jace opened his eyes. "You're serious, aren't you?"

"Yes." She'd lain awake and thought about this for a long time last night. "My former roommate says Barry threatened to kill me. To kill Kat," Katy amended, struggling to keep this confusing perspective straight. "Suppose he came out here and in a fit of fury *did it*. He dashes back to New York, calls out here a few times to keep tabs on what's going on, and then gets the shock of his life when I, identifying myself as Kat, answer the phone. So he rushes out here to take a look at me, and

186

when he sees I really do look like the real Kat, he decides he can solve all his problems by making a model out of *me*."

Jace considered her scenario, then shook his head. "Big problem with that. Mrs. L. took you into Redding to meet your friends *after* Barry went back to New York."

"*If* he went back to New York immediately after leaving the ranch."

Jace's smooth forehead wrinkled. "Katy, what are you saying? That he could have come back and killed her, which makes it premeditated murder, and, while he was carrying her body into the woods to hide it, her necklace got caught on a bush?"

"What better place to dispose of a body? Jace, while Barry was here, he went for a walk in the woods by himself. He came back with gooey mud all over his shoes. I came home with the same kind of mud on my shoes when I got lost out there and found the necklace! Maybe Barry went back to check on where he'd hidden the body."

Jace shook his head and patted her cheek. "Katy, hon, I think you've been reading too many murder mysteries. There are muddy little springs scattered all over the woods here. We had a terrible mess when the boys found one and got in a mud fight last spring."

"I haven't read a single murder mystery," Katy said defensively, unhappily aware that she'd apparently lost him when she plunged into the mud clue. Until then he'd seemed to see a certain logic in her suspicions. "I've been reading my mother's old children's books." She paused, a loop in her convoluted thinking now twisting back on her, this one a dismaying consequence that hadn't occurred to her before. "If she is my mother."

"Katy."

"You really think I've lost it, don't you?"

He hesitated. "I can see how in such a peculiar situation as this that peculiar possibilities might occur to us. But the idea that the real Kat was murdered and you're someone else who looks exactly like her and just happened to get amnesia at the right time to step into her shoes, well, you have to admit it's pretty far-fetched."

"We don't need to tell anyone, but we could, you know, just look around out in the woods," she suggested tentatively.

"And you could, you know, lighten up and get a little more rest and sleep." He smiled as he repeated her uncertain phrasing. "And maybe, you know, not let your imagination run away with you?"

Katy nodded reluctantly. Yes, what she was suggesting *was* far-fetched, and she often didn't sleep well, and sometimes her imagination did jump into overdrive. And the suspicions of someone who couldn't even remember her own past had all the credibility of a tabloid article about UFO abductions and alien babies. And yet...

Katy went to bed that night determined to simply stop thinking all these wild thoughts. Yet they churned around as if caught in some endless spin cycle.

Because, if she ignored the "far-outness" of the possibility that she wasn't Katy Cavanaugh, that she was someone else, it all fit. Barry's astonishment on that first phone call. His version of past events, so calculatedly different from Stephanie's. The differences between Katy's personality and the past Kat's personality. Barry, with his fury over her dumping him both personally and professionally, had the motive to kill Kat and the observed bursts of violent temper to do it.

Had Barry earlier congratulated himself on the amazing

coincidence that Mrs. L. had accidentally produced a double to solve his problems? Was he now nervous because the necklace had turned up? He wouldn't want to acknowledge remembering the necklace if he now realized it had been around Kat's neck when he killed her.

And now, viewed from a different perspective, Barry's eagerness for Katy to come to New York took on new and ominous undertones. Was his real motive in wanting her in New York so that he could keep an eye on her in case her memory returned and his whole scheme collapsed in inevitable questions about what had happened to the real Kat?

No, she realized with a shiver in spite of the warm night, Barry couldn't let it go that far. He would have to keep people from ever realizing Kat Cavanaugh was missing. If some unfortunate New York "accident" happened to *this* Katy Cavanaugh, there would never be any dangerous questions or investigation about a missing person. Kat Cavanaugh would simply be dead. And Barry Alexander would be home free.

If he had killed once, he could kill again.

Well, take care of that, she thought shakily, by simply staying far, far away from Barry and New York. As of right now, any thought of returning to New York was canceled.

But just before sleep, another odd thought prickled the perimeter of her consciousness: Jace had also been shocked and astonished that first time she'd talked with him on the phone. Kat? he'd said incredulously. *Kat?* And he'd also been shocked to learn the necklace was found in the woods....

Seventeen

S hadows. Now she's seeing shadows.

He paced the room restlessly, seeing shadows of his own. Winter moonlight shafting through the trees as he carried the body deep into the woods. Slogging through wet, sloppy patches of snow, the metal-handled shovel icy in his hand. Heavy mud coating his shoes and weighing down his pants legs as he dug. Water seeping into the bottom of the narrow pit and making a soggy splash when he dropped her in. The sodden thud of clods of dirt hitting the body.

He broke out in a sweat, but this was not like the hot sweat of exertion that had poured off him that night. This was a cold sweat of anger and apprehension.

Everything had been going so great. She'd stepped into Kat's shoes as if she'd been born in them. He'd thought he had it made.

But now, shadows. And the necklace. How had she stumbled onto that? Eighty acres of ranch, and she heads like a homing pigeon for that particular spot.

Where she'd found the necklace wasn't necessarily where the body was buried, however, he reminded himself. He must remain calm so he could think clearly and not plunge into some disastrous mistake. The necklace could have been ripped off anywhere out in that jungle of brush and trees. So, even if she somehow found her way back to the spot, she wouldn't necessarily be at the site of the body.

Forget the necklace. It was a minor detail. What mattered were those dangerous shadows lurking in her head. He couldn't afford to wait until they exploded into real memories of some other identity and life. Because that was when a whole new can of worms would fly open. Questions about where was the real Kat, why had no one ever heard from her, when and where was she last seen, who she was with, all that garbage.

Everything, he thought resentfully, would have worked out so great if the new Kat's memory had just stayed buried, if she had simply become Kat Cavanaugh. But she couldn't just leave the past alone. No, she had to keep probing and examining and digging, not nearly so sweet and nice as he'd once thought.

He'd never intended to kill the real Kat, of course. But she'd driven him to it. She'd made it happen. They could have had such a fantastic life together! He could have dumped the charade he was running here and become her full-time manager. And husband. His hands twitched and flexed with savage, bitter memory of what had really happened. How she'd scornfully rejected his love and laughed and made fun of him. Oh yes, she deserved what she got.

Now he had this to deal with. Because the new Kat's memory was returning, no doubt about it. He wondered about her sometimes, who she was, where she'd come from, how she'd wound up on that beach in Oregon, why no one seemed to care that she was missing. But none of that really mattered.

What mattered was that she had to die. Soon. While she and everyone else still believed she was Katy Cavanaugh.

It wouldn't be so difficult after all. His fists clenched. He was angry with her now. Women. Always troublemakers.

Katy made the request in a phone call just a day later, early in the morning. She knew her request would puzzle and disturb Dr. Fischer, and she was right.

"Is something wrong, Katy?" the doctor asked with instant concern.

"No, I don't think so. I was just hoping you could check on

192

this for me, because it would be difficult and awkward to do here."

"Is it from your memory? Is anything coming back yet?"

"Just a few odd shadows. Nothing recognizable. I'll let you know if there's any real breakthrough."

Dr. Fischer hesitated, as if she wanted to pry further, but finally she simply said, "Okay, then, you want me to go to Police Chief Derrickson and find out if any missing person reports have ever come in that match your description. From anywhere in the country."

"Right. Or descriptions of fugitive criminals that match it," Katy added, thinking there was also that unpleasant possibility. A past written in invisible ink could have anything in it.

Dr. Fischer, ever shrewd, cut straight to the core. "Do you have some reason to doubt you *are* Katy Cavanaugh?"

"I'm not sure. I guess I just want to cover all bases."

Dr. Fischer called back that evening. The Benton Beach police department had no missing-person or criminal-fugitive reports about anyone matching her description.

So there was a big hole in her maybe-I'm-not-Katy-Cavanaugh theory, she thought as she hung up the phone. After all this time, if there *was* a missing "Jane Doe from Denver," or "Judy Jones from Juneau," someone surely would have reported it. She couldn't simply have dropped into a hole in space and time and been forgotten by everyone.

Firmly she decided this was all a big relief. Mrs. L. hadn't made a mistake in identifying her. Barry wasn't a premeditated murderer, but simply a slick opportunist who had seen an unexpected chance to use her lost memory to rewrite the past and improve his situation both personally and professionally.

She *was* Kat "Katy" Cavanaugh, she had a garden-variety amnesia, and she'd simply have to wait for her memory to return. And her momentary suspicion about Jace, *Jace* of all people, was paranoia at its wildest.

She didn't see Jace for a couple of days, but she attended services with him in the chapel on Sunday. After dinner he asked if she'd like to ride down to Redding with him and several of the boys the following day. Katy jumped at the opportunity. Maybe it would take her mind away from all the wild suspicions that nibbled like hungry predators at the edges of her mind.

The van, with Joe driving, picked her up early the following morning. Joe invited Mrs. L. to come along, but she declined. She hadn't been feeling well for several days and said she thought she'd just spend the day resting and napping.

Definitely a good thing Mrs. L. hadn't come along, Katy decided long before they reached Redding. The van's automatic transmission was acting up, and sometimes the shift from gear to gear came with a neck-snapping lurch. The boys didn't misbehave, Jace would never have allowed that, but they were boys: noisy, teasing, laughing, squabbling. They got thirsty, had to go to the bathroom, argued the merits of various teams and athletes, sneaked in sly punches and pinches.

Jace grinned as a surreptitious burping contest erupted. "How about you? Want a herd of kids of your own?"

For a moment an inexplicable shudder of pain rolled through her, as sharp as if she'd been ambushed with a blow to the back of the head. It was so shocking, so unexpected, so *blinding*, that she momentarily reeled with it. She clutched the arm rest to steady herself. Kat Cavanaugh had never suffered

194

any pain connected with a child. Why had this innocuous question hit her so hard? But if she *wasn't* Kat...

No. She'd been down that dead-end road before. *Get it through your stitched-up head,* she commanded herself roughly, *you are Kat Cavanaugh.* Quickly she turned to mischief-eyed Ramsey. "Knock, knock," she said.

He grinned as if they'd been telling each other jokes for years. "Who's there?"

And as the silly jokes flew back and forth, Katy set aside that peculiar jolt of pain and smiled an answer to Jace's question. Yes, she wanted children. Energetic, teasing, laughing, ever-into-mischief, squabbling children. Oh, yes!

They were all still laughing when they arrived at the medical clinic, but Katy's laughter suddenly froze. Jace slid the door of the van open, and the boys piled out. Jace leaned back inside, making arrangements with Joe about when to pick them up. He glanced at Katy, who was still staring at the clinic building.

"Look familiar?" he asked.

No, not familiar, but some peculiar sense of recognition flowed through her. A faint medicinal scent, a woman in a white lab coat hurrying out the door, an invisible aura of busy, modern medical technology.

The shadows—no, a single shadow—moved inside her head again. It was the smallest figure, with head bowed, crying, crying. Katy didn't understand, but tears filled her own eyes, and panic trembled in her heart.

"Katy, Katy!" Jace shook her lightly. She blinked and swallowed. "Shadows?"

She nodded dumbly. He glanced at the boys waiting outside, as if he were being pulled in two directions.

She patted his arm. "You go on and take care of the boys." By now she knew the reason for this trip. Each of these boys had a medical problem needing special attention. Ramsey's was a slightly deformed foot that should have been treated when he was a baby but could possibly still be corrected by surgery. The other boys had problems ranging from severe allergy attacks to a potentially serious heart murmur. "It's faded away now."

Joe dropped Katy at a shopping mall across town, and she enjoyed the morning wandering through the stores even though her mind kept slipping back to those brief moments outside the clinic. She bought silky flowered material and yarn for Mrs. L., a couple of books for herself, and bubble gum for the boys. She didn't intend to get anything special for Jace, but a certain rakish straw hat looked so perfect that she couldn't resist buying it.

Mrs. L. hadn't been able to remember the name of the restaurant to which she'd taken Katy to meet her friend or friends in Redding, but she'd thought it had "mountain" in it. Katy searched the restaurant listings in a phone book but found nothing that sounded likely, and she finally abandoned her earlier idea of trying to jog her memory by visiting the restaurant. Her memory had already been jogged today. But what did it mean?

Joe picked her up about one o'clock at the agreed-upon mall entrance. Jace met the van at the door of the medical center and said the boys wouldn't be through for another fifteen or twenty minutes yet. He went back inside, and Joe parked the van on the shady side of the parking lot. Katy didn't mind the wait. The temperature outside must have been over a hundred, but the air-conditioned van was cool and comfortable. She offered Joe an old-fashioned lemon drop from the sack she'd bought at a candy shop.

Making idle conversation she asked, "Have you been with the school long?"

"I knew Jace back in his football days. I worked for the last team he was with, taking care of the uniforms and equipment. Until I got fired for drinking and messing up on the job once too often."

Katy glanced at Joe in surprise. That he wasn't an educated man was fairly obvious, but he was so reliable, and the school depended on him for so much that she'd never have guessed this darker past.

He smiled, as if he could read her mind. "Most of the guys on the team looked on me like I was just another piece of broken-down equipment, but Jace was always good to me. And if it weren't for him, I'd sure be homeless or in jail or dead by now."

"Getting this job changed you?"

Joe shook his head vehemently. "No. The Lord changed Jace, and Jace came looking for me. He dragged me out to the ranch, sobered me up, and gave me the job. Then he introduced me to the Lord, and the *Lord* changed me. Because he cares."

What Jace's friend had done for him, Jace had done for someone else, Katy mused. Like an endless chain of God's love and caring.

If you wanted to believe in a loving, caring God, she thought scornfully, her familiar resentment rising like an angry buzz saw to break that naïve "chain of God's love and caring" thought.

"I guess I'd do most anything for Jace," Joe added as he selected another lemon drop. He spoke as casually as if he were commenting on the weather, but Katy heard the immovable depths of bedrock loyalty in the simple statement.

"And Mrs. L.?" she asked lightly.

Joe grinned self-consciously, even a hint of embarrassed

color rising to his leathery old cheeks. "Lenore's a fine woman."

Delighted by the unexpected blush, Katy couldn't resist a bit of teasing. "Maybe we'll hear wedding bells one of these days?"

"Well, I don't know about *that.*"

Joe's hasty sidestep surprised Katy. Did it mean he didn't actually want to marry Mrs. L., or the other way around? She couldn't ask such a rude question, of course, but Joe unexpectedly volunteered a bit of information.

"Evan would have to approve before Lenore'd do it, of course, and I guess the truth is that there's no love lost between Evan and me."

That comment also surprised Katy. What she personally knew of Evan came only from her long phone conversations with him, but he'd been wonderfully warm and friendly and patient with her. "That's too bad. He's been so nice to me, talking about our childhood together and trying to help me remember."

Joe shrugged his bony shoulders. "Memories aren't so great. Sometimes we'd be better off without 'em."

An odd observation, Katy thought, but all she said was, "Did you and Evan have some disagreement?"

"No, not really. I never actually said anything to him because I didn't want to make Lenore mad, but I'm sure he knows I figure he takes advantage of her."

"But he calls her often and comes to see her whenever he can," Katy protested. "That's more than a lot of sons do."

"Well, I'm pretty sure he latched onto most of the money your folks left Lenore, and I don't think that's right. They wanted to make her old age secure, not supply Evan with the money to buy some expensive car. Have you ever priced a Porsche 911?"

"But Evan didn't get the money," Katy said quickly. "Mrs. L. had an elderly aunt who needed an expensive organ transplant, and that's where it went. You know what a generous and caring person she is. And Evan is a very successful businessman. I'm sure he can afford to buy his own expensive car."

"I didn't know anything about the sick aunt," Joe conceded. He tilted his head, as if he were still skeptical, but then he nodded slowly. "But it sounds like something Lenore'd do, all right."

"And she wouldn't be one to brag about her generosity."

"I guess Evan probably isn't such a bad sort." Joe grinned ruefully. "Maybe he's never been too fond of me because he figures I'm just some ex-alcoholic old gold digger out to take advantage of his mother."

Katy smiled and impulsively reached over to squeeze his arm. "I'll put in a good word for you."

His sideways glance was teasing. "I've already put in a few good words for you. Though I don't really think you need 'em."

They went to a fast-food taco stand for lunch. It was busy and crowded, and the boys, tired of being cooped up in the medical clinic for hours, clamored to eat outside at a picnic table on the patio. The heat was already getting to Katy, and she bypassed the outdoor eating area and headed for the van with her burrito and 7UP. On the way she had to step aside to keep from almost getting run over by a trio of shaved-headed guys wearing baggy pants and sloppy T-shirts emblazoned with cartoonish figures of overdeveloped women. The swaggering eighteen- or nineteen-years-olds, with muscles bulging from the ripped-armhole T-shirts, instantly made Katy uneasy, but she reminded herself that people shouldn't be judged by clothing and appearance. Just because these three *looked* like outlaw teen-gang hoodlums didn't mean they were. After all, not so long ago she'd had a shaved head herself.

Then one of the boys made such a lewd remark to her that her face burned. So much for being nonjudgmental, she fumed as she hurried on to the van. They *were* a minigang of hoodlums. At the door, she glanced back to see where the three toughs were headed.

They took the picnic table next to Jace and Joe and the boys. In the process of climbing to sit on the tabletop, feet on the bench, one guy knocked off the new straw hat Katy had just given Jace. It could have been an accident, but Katy didn't think so. She clutched her soft drink container so hard that it slopped 7UP on her pants, uneasy about a situation that suddenly looked ominous. Jace, however, simply picked up the hat and placed it in his lap while he bowed his head to offer the before-meal prayer. One of the toughs must have made some nasty crack during the prayer because Ramsey's head jerked up, his expression startled. Jace must also have heard the remark, but he didn't let on. He simply finished the prayer and started distributing hamburgers and tacos.

Katy relaxed slightly and climbed into the van. Although the three guys were obviously psyched for trouble, Jace didn't intend to accommodate them. She ate more hurriedly than usual, and suspected the boys did too. They piled their trash on a couple of trays, and Ramsey and another boy started toward the trash container carrying them.

The toughs stood up, one of them making an elaborate, macho display of squashing their three drink cartons together. He casually planted the cartons on Ramsey's tray. Ramsey offered no objection and continued on to the trash container, but the tray accidentally tilted and the crumpled cartons slid off. The tough sneered something and shoved Ramsey toward the fallen cartons. The tray crashed, and the small, slight boy tumbled to the concrete patio. Horrified, Katy saw the guy's big hand close around Ramsey's head, as if he were going to yank the boy to his feet by the hair.

So fast that Katy hardly knew how it happened, Jace grabbed the guy, swung him around, and smashed a fist into his face. The kid reeled groggily but shook his head like an outraged bull and roared back as if he'd just been waiting for a chance to launch an all-out brawl. He crashed a fist low in Jace's midsection, followed it with a solid blow to his eye. But even as brawny, tough, and mean-tempered as the big kid was, he was no match for Jace's fury and maturity and hard experience. A moment later he plunged to his knees, arms clamped over his ears as he uselessly tried to protect his head from Jace's savage blows. One of his friends jumped into the fray, but with no more than a contemptuous glance Jace smashed a kick into the guy's groin, a blow that even Katy recognized as down-and-dirty street-brawl technique. The guy howled in pain and sank to his knees, and Jace hammered another blow into the side of the first one's head.

Katy, who had been sitting there welded to her seat, screamed as she realized Jace had lost it, that he was out of control. She rammed the sliding door of the van open. "Joe, stop him, *stop him!*"

Joe was already behind Jace, desperately trying to wrestle his arms behind him and pull him off his downed opponent.

"Jace!" Katy screamed. "*Jace!*"

She knew he didn't hear her. His murderous fog shut out everything but his fury as he hammered blow after blow like some relentless battering machine, Joe's arms binding him no more than twine on a wild horse. The young tough was flat on his back now, Jace straddling him, the guy's bleeding nose slanted at an impossible angle. Jace raised a fist to deliver a final blow to his opponent's fading consciousness.

Then he stopped. He leaned back on his heels and looked

at his hands as if they were strangers. He stumbled to his feet and backed away, shaking his head as if coming out of a daze. The young tough frantically crawled away, leaving a trail of blood from his shattered nose.

People were gathering now, asking each other what was going on, and someone yelled to get the police. Katy pushed her way through the crowd. Heat waves shimmered on the hot concrete. The drops of blood shone like evil jewels. "We need a doctor!" she cried.

The three young toughs were not waiting for medical attention. The two manhandled their buddy to his feet and half walked, half dragged him to an old blue car at the curb. They screeched off in a burning squeal of tires. Jace shook his head when Joe asked if he needed a doctor.

A police car arrived. Jace was up front about what had happened, that he'd thrown the first blow, but Ramsey's bloody knees and scraped hands attested to why Jace had defended him. With the three guys gone, no neutral bystanders clear about what had happened, and no one interested in pressing charges against anyone else, the police finally just told everyone to disperse.

Jace went to the restroom to clean up. Joe, visibly sagging, herded the boys to the van. Katy slid into the front seat beside Joe. He clutched the steering wheel in what she knew was an effort to hold his hands steady. The boys huddled in their seats, uncharacteristically subdued, obviously shocked by what had just happened. But no more shocked than Katy.

Ramsey came up to peer between the seats. "I didn't mean to cause trouble."

"It wasn't your fault." Katy squeezed his arm reassuringly. She reached into one of her bags and handed him a fistful of bubble gum. "Here. Pass this around. Everything's okay now."

She glanced at Joe, the unspoken question in her eyes: *was* everything okay now?

Joe nodded, but Katy wasn't convinced.

"Joe, what happened here?" she asked, her whisper frantic but pitched low so the boys in back couldn't hear. "Do things like this happen often?"

"No!" Katy heard the fierce protectiveness in Joe's voice. "Nothing like this has happened for a long time."

"But it has happened before?"

Joe hesitated, his long, appraising look doing nothing to calm her nerves. She almost felt as if *she* were on trial as he studied her. Finally he said, "I guess you were never a football fan."

"I wouldn't remember it if I were. I have amnesia," she reminded him bluntly.

Joe's bony hands flexed around the steering wheel. "Jace had a lot of trouble with his temper back in his football days," he said reluctantly.

"On the field or off?"

"Both. Once, when he was mad about some illegal stuff the referee missed in a game, he stormed into the opposing team's locker room and took out half a dozen guys before the rest of the team brought him down. He got in barroom and street fights and had run-ins with referees and TV cameramen. The sports reporters took to calling him Fast-Fist Foster. Once he spent a week in jail for punching out a sportscaster who made some comments he didn't like. He got fined or suspended from the team I don't know how many times. But he was such an outstanding player that he got away with it for quite a while. Another team was always willing to take a chance on him. But eventually, after he hurt his knee..."

Joe's low-spoken words trailed off, but Katy understood. By

then, with a bad knee, Jace was more trouble than he was worth. She leaned back in her seat, shocked. Jace had told her he had a temper, even that it had been a part of why he'd left professional football. But she had never realized how raw that temper was or what a decisive factor it had been in his leaving football.

"But that was all a long time ago," Joe said fiercely. "He found the Lord and he changed. Today was just a onetime thing, and you can't blame him for protecting Ramsey."

Katy could believe Jace was indeed on a longer fuse than he had been back in those hard-brawling days. She had seen his good-natured patience with the boys. She had today seen him ignore the harassment of offensive taunts and having his hat knocked off. Yet under the strain of the injustices against Ramsey his temper had finally exploded.

She could understand and even sympathize with his anger today. She'd lost her tolerant attitude toward the three guys the instant she heard the lewd remark directed at her. But the savage fury of Jace's reaction when his temper finally snapped, the violence of it!

Maybe it hadn't happened for years, as Joe claimed.

And maybe, she thought with a shiver in spite of the heat, it had. In her mind's eye, she saw the florid wine stain on a bedroom carpet.

Joe scowled at her lack of response, but all he said was, "And you can bet, if this was the old days, he wouldn't have backed off when he did. But now, God spoke to him, and he quit. Just like that. You can also bet he's talking to God about all this right now, asking for his forgiveness and help. And one or two slips don't cancel out all the good Jace is doing." Again his voice was low and fierce.

One *or two* slips. What did that mean?

Jace yanked the door of the van open. His hair glistened

wetly, as if he'd held his head under the cold water in the restroom. Both his eye and upper lip were already swollen, the eye darkening. He slid into the seat behind Joe.

"You can sit up here," Katy offered.

"No, this is fine." He jerked his head to signal Joe to head for home, then slumped forward with his head in his hands.

Katy rubbed a shaky hand across her forehead when they finally reached the freeway. Her hand came away wet with the perspiration running down her face, and sweat welded her blouse to her back. She realized now that the van was no longer cool. It was, in fact, a moving oven. Joe whipped the air-conditioner controls back and forth, but nothing happened.

"It's on the blink again." He slammed his palm against the vent in frustration. "I'll have to look at it soon as we can find a rest area. Though what we probably need is a whole new air-conditioning system."

Jace leaned between the seats, but his manipulation of the controls was no more effective than Joe's. "What we need is a whole new van," he muttered.

They opened all the windows, but the moving air was only a blast of searing wind, and heat boiled up through the floorboards from the sizzling freeway. Katy slipped off her shoes and swabbed her face with a tissue, going more limp by the moment.

At the rest area the few shady parking spots were already taken, and Joe had to park the van in the open sun.

"You okay?" Jace leaned forward to ask Katy.

She nodded, although she felt rather less than *okay*. The shock of what had happened in Redding, the heat, the taco-stand salsa burning like an open campfire in her stomach, the strange, apprehensive thoughts about Jace swirling like some ominous abstract painting in her head...

He squeezed her shoulder. "I'm sorry, Katy."

What was he apologizing for? Inviting her along? the heat? the broken air-conditioner? what he'd done today? what he'd done in the past? *What he might yet do in the future if his temper snapped again?*

Eighteen

Jace set Katy's shopping bags by the door. With an odd detachment, Katy watched her own hand tremble as she reached for the doorknob.

He put his hand over hers. "Please don't be upset with Joe. He feels terrible about what happened. He couldn't see you and had no idea you were behind the van. He thought you'd gone to the ladies' room."

Joe had apologized. Profusely. But it wasn't his frantic apology that now echoed in Katy's ears. It was his earlier words. *I guess I'd do most anything for Jace.* Had he almost done something for Jace today?

No. *No!* Of course not. That kind of thinking was wild and irrational and paranoid. Heat wilting body and mind, salsa flaming in her stomach, bruised body aching, shock rattling her nerves—she just wasn't thinking straight. Because if she thought what had happened today at the rest area was *not* an accident...

Again she rejected that wild thought and its shattering implications.

Mrs. L. opened the door before Katy could turn the knob. She looked pale, obviously still not feeling up to par, her usually neat gray hair untidy, but her concern was all for Katy. "Katy, sweetie, what happened to you?" she gasped.

Katy's fingers automatically went to the raw scrape on her chin. Mrs. L. leaned over and gasped at the blur of tire tracks on Katy's loose shirttail and the smudges of asphalt on her pants.

Jace answered for Katy. "Little mishap. I thought she should see a doctor, but she refused, so I did what I could with the first-aid kit. Let's get her inside. We've been sweltering without air conditioning all afternoon."

Jace's strong grip on Katy's upper arm guided her to the breakfast nook. The house felt deliciously cool, a log bubble of paradise. It almost made her aching body feel less battered and bruised.

"Katy, I'm sorry," Jace said again. "It's been a terrible day for you. I have to get the boys home now, but I'll check on you later, okay?"

Katy nodded and a few moments later heard a spurt of gravel as the van lurched out of the driveway, the transmission still jerky. Mrs. L. brought her a glass of iced tea and a flood of questions.

"Katy, what *happened?* Your face is all skinned up, and your elbow, too! But you always were one to get all scraped up."

Without waiting for answers she bustled off to collect a basin of hot water and first-aid supplies, and while she cleaned and disinfected and applied ointment, Katy told her what had happened. As best she could. Everything was a little blurred, as if heat waves still shimmered in her head.

They'd stopped at the rest area, and Joe had jumped out to look at the air-conditioning unit. Jace distributed soft drinks from the ice chest, and the boys raced for the shade. Katy took one but couldn't drink it, her stomach still queasy. Jace followed the boys. Katy sat glued to the hot vinyl seat, needing to use the restroom but dreading the scorching walk to it.

Finally she psyched herself up for it. It was a long step out of the van, and her leg wobbled when her foot hit the asphalt. Joe's head was buried in the engine compartment. She had to go around behind the van to get to the restroom, but she suddenly felt dizzy, as if her stomach might go into full rebellion.

She slumped weakly against the rear bumper.

A few moments later the van's engine started, but before Katy could move, the van jerked backward. She lost the details then. Hot black asphalt rising to meet her. Hands and knees and chin hitting the harsh surface. Tumbling, rolling, kaleidoscope of blue sky and blazing sun and forested hillside. Monster of the van looming over her, huge tires, the jagged black ruts of the tread filling the landscape of her vision, sure knowledge that she was about to be crushed.

Screams and yells, strong hands pulling her to safety.

"Jace pulled you out of the way before the van could run over you?"

No. Not Jace. A middle-aged stranger who'd seen a disaster about to happen had hammered on the van to stop Joe, then grabbed Katy and dragged her to the grass.

Jace came running then. So did the boys and Joe and more strangers, everyone peering down at her as if she were inside some strange flower with petals of human faces. She remembered Joe leaning over her, leathery skin ashen, stammering a distraught apology. "I didn't know you were back there! A parking space opened up, and I was just going to move the van over in the shade!" Jace bringing the first-aid kit and a glass of cold water.

"Well, my goodness, I know Joe's been grumbling about the van, but how could he have been so careless!" Mrs. L. exclaimed, her tone vexed.

Careless? Or calculated? If that stranger hadn't seen what was happening...

Mrs. L. made a cool, refreshing fruit salad for supper. Katy told the housekeeper about her peculiar reaction to the medical clinic and the reappearance of a single crying shadow, but Mrs. L. doubted it was meaningful.

"More likely just some subconscious reminder of the hospital in Oregon where you regained consciousness," she suggested, and Katy, on reflection, decided that could be true. Perhaps the crying figure was simply herself, lost and alone.

Mrs. L. put Katy to bed with a sleeping pill. "Nothing powerful, just a little something I use when I can't sleep. And I'll just have a word with Joe. That man is going to get a piece of *my* mind!"

Katy heard vague, diluted sounds before she drifted off to sleep. The little click the bedroom phone made when the other phone was used. The sound of a car engine. Voices. Mrs. L. scolding Joe? Jace checking on her? It all seemed oddly distant.

By morning, when she showered, she found an impressive display of bruises on her body. She still ached all over, and the sleeping pill had left her feeling sluggish both physically and mentally.

Jace came over that evening. Katy was stretched out on the sofa in the living room, and Mrs. L. let him in. His eye was smoky black now, but he somehow looked attractively mysterious rather than blemished. And, even with a puffy upper lip, he could still win any handsome-hunks contest, she thought with a little catch of breath.

He handed her a folded sheet of heavy blue paper. "The boys made this for you."

It was a clever get-well card they had made on the computer. Katy laughed at the instantly identifiable cartoon figure of herself they had managed to create, tall and lanky, with bright yellow, close-cropped hair and a slightly cross-eyed expression. "Tell them I appreciate it very much."

He took off the new straw hat and dropped into a cross-legged position on the floor beside her.

"Is Ramsey okay?" she asked. "His knees and hands also took a beating."

"Ramsey's fine." He tenderly ran his knuckles along the line of her jaw, carefully skirting the scraped area on her chin. They small-talked about the patch-up work Joe had done on the van's transmission today and how fast the boys were progressing on the new computers. Mrs. L. brought iced tea and cookies. Finally Jace smiled ruefully. "I guess we can't avoid talking about it indefinitely, can we?"

"Talking about what?" As if she didn't know.

"What happened yesterday."

"It wasn't entirely unwarranted. If you hadn't jumped in, that big thug might have done worse than he did to Ramsey. I have a feeling the N word came into it somewhere, too?"

Jace nodded. "But that's no excuse. There are better ways to handle ugly situations than beating the pulp out of someone."

Katy ran a fingertip along the folded edge of the card. Without looking at him she asked, "When was the last time something like this happened?"

"Events during my drinking, brawling days are a little hazy, but I think it was in Denver when some guy crowded into a parking space I was headed for. It didn't take much to set me off back then. I'm ashamed of those days," he added flatly. "And I'm not proud of yesterday's miserable exhibition, either."

"Christians aren't perfect, just forgiven." She said the words absentmindedly, without thinking, then realized Jace was staring at her perplexedly. She shrugged defensively. "I guess I must have heard that somewhere."

"I wonder where."

"Maybe I saw it on a T-shirt. Or a bumper sticker." She felt defensive, as she always did when one of these unlikely statements popped out of her.

He twisted the beginning of a curl of her blond hair around

his finger. "Katy, I don't know what to do about you."

She raised up on one elbow, vaguely alarmed. "*Do* about me? What do you mean?"

"I'm falling in love with you. And I'm not sure that's a good idea."

She dropped back to the cushion, emotions jumbled by this mixed message about his feelings. "Not a good idea because I don't share your Christian commitment? Or not a good idea because of my memory problems? Or maybe because you remember what I was like before?" She paused reflectively. "That's a rather daunting list, isn't it?"

"I'm falling anyway. Actually, I guess I might as well admit it. I've already fallen." He leaned over and kissed the tip of her nose. His puffy lip felt strange but not unpleasant against her skin. His face hovered over hers, as if he were torn between wanting to kiss her, a kiss that went far beyond a brush of lips on the nose, and thinking that wasn't a good idea. She smoothed the heavy line of his left eyebrow. "You're not saying anything," he finally added lightly. "Do you have a daunting list of your own?"

She nodded slowly, not elaborating on the list even to herself. "But I'm falling in love, too."

They looked at each other, studying, wondering, as if a door had opened between them but neither was sure about stepping through.

"Shall we just leave it at that for the moment?" Jace finally said huskily. "And see where the Lord leads us?"

Instant retorts shot across her mind. *What did the Lord have to do with this? He just sits up in his heaven and doesn't care!* But she left the words unspoken, at least for the moment, and just nodded. Jace kissed her again, gently, on the forehead.

~ ~ ~ ~ ~

After Jace left, Katy turned out the lights and went outside to sit on the deck. The house was silent. Mrs. L., after peeking into the living room to say she had a headache, had already gone to bed. The boards in the deck and the wooden lounge chair still held the warmth of the day, pleasant against Katy's skin and bare feet in the sweet coolness of the night. The crickets still sang their insistent chorus, punctuated by the deep croaks of the frogs, but she wasn't thinking about the 'cricket' puzzle tonight. She gazed up at the stars without really seeing their spangled radiance, her thoughts looking inward.

One part of her soared joyously with Jace's declaration of love. She clasped it to her heart and danced with it. But another part peered behind the statement with cynical doubt. *Was* he in love with her? Or was this some calculated attempt to distract her, to put her off guard?

Off guard from what?

She rose restlessly from the chair and leaned against the wooden railing, hands clasped. Okay, no more tiptoeing around. Time to face these insidious little doubts and suspicions squarely.

It all went back, of course, to the nagging doubt about her real identity, that maybe she *wasn't* Kat Cavanaugh. A different past life was like a blank television screen; she had nothing but those shadowy figures to fill it. But the danger, if there was danger, wasn't in the blank screen of that other life. The danger was here, tied to an unanswerable question: if she wasn't Kat Cavanaugh, where was the real Kat?

The fact that another Kat, if she existed, hadn't been heard from in all these months definitely suggested that something had happened to her. It wasn't logical that she'd simply abandon the ranch and other financial assets and disappear indefinitely.

Which brought Barry into the picture.

He had motive to kill the real Kat for dumping him both personally and professionally, and, in a flash of anger that certainly made violence appear possible, he'd threatened to do it. He'd lied to Katy and tried to deceive her about what had happened in New York. He had much to gain if an accidental substitute became the real Kat and stepped into her modeling and fiancée shoes. He had much to lose if the substitute remembered she was someone else. And danger of discovery that he'd murdered the real Kat could be averted if the substitute conveniently died while everyone thought she was the real Kat.

Yes, she had reason to believe Barry posed a real threat. But he was three thousand miles away, and he couldn't hurt her from there. He'd had nothing to do with what had almost happened on the trip to Redding.

Jace, however, was right here.

But there was no reason to be suspicious of Jace! It was unfair to be suspicious of Jace. Jace loved her. She loved him!

Yet he had been so astonished that first time she called him when she was flat on her back in the bedroom. As astonished as if he were hearing from someone who'd come back from the dead. Which, if he knew the real Kat was dead, would certainly have been how it would have felt to him.

He'd explained his reaction, of course: surprise that Kat would call him after the ugly scene they'd had. But was that enough to justify the intensity of his astonishment at the call?

But why would Jace have killed Kat? Was fury over her refusal to go through with the land deal enough to make him snap? Or could there have been something more? That wine stain on the bedroom carpet...

Like an arrow shot to the far side of a primitive battle, her mind suddenly jumped to a different perspective from what Jace had told her about that night.

Suppose Kat hadn't tried to seduce Jace there in the bedroom. Suppose it was the other way around. Jace trying to seduce Kat, or even trying to force himself on her! Now Katy saw a vision shockingly different from the one Jace had painted for her.

Kat rejecting Jace, desperately flinging the wine at him to drive him off, Jace reacting in violent fury! The same savage fury he'd shown with that bully in Redding. Her heart hammered, and her hands clenched the rail until her fingers cramped.

Then her perspective somersaulted again, and she swallowed in relief. No, that couldn't have happened.

It couldn't have happened because Mrs. L. had driven Kat into Redding, and Kat was alive and well then, which was at least several days after the bedroom scene. And Barry's visit had also occurred after the bedroom incident. Which brought her back to the probability that if something had happened to the real Kat, Barry, not Jace, had been involved.

Unless Jace had followed and done something to her after Mrs. L. dropped her off in Redding.

She shivered with another unexpected vision: Jace furtively stealing through the woods with Kat's body hanging over his shoulder, the necklace accidentally snagging on a bush, glittering unnoticed in a patch of moonlight.

She abandoned that appalling vision, rejecting it almost fiercely. She loved Jace. He was the only secure haven she had, her place of refuge! Jace couldn't be a murderer!

Why not? The question rose with cynical detachment. Did her love make him innocent? No. Did Christian faith, or a *profession* of Christian faith, even a multitude of good works, make commitment of a crime impossible? No. Just read the newspapers, she thought grimly.

And there was Joe. Faithful, loyal Joe. Yesterday's mishap

could have been the accident it appeared to be. But what if Joe knew Jace had killed the real Kat? What if he saw the danger of the substitute Kat's memory returning? What if he saw a way to protect Jace by getting rid of that substitute before anyone knew she wasn't the real thing? Jace might even have *suggested* that a helpful little accident would be much appreciated.

I guess I'd do most anything for Jace.

She rubbed her forehead, the sullen squeeze of a headache clamping around her temples. It was all so complicated, so confusing. So terrifying. She turned her face up to the stars, closing her eyes to look inside and inspect that word.

Yes. *Terrifying.*

Terrifying because she was in love with Jace and didn't trust him.

An all-encompassing feeling of aloneness infiltrated her as she stood there under the bloodless, distant glitter of the stars. The aloneness seeped through her skin and into her bones and surrounded her heart. No one to talk to, no one to confide in, no one she could ask, *Am I imagining things, seeing monsters and villains where none exist? Am I just a little crazy?* No one to comfort or guide or cherish her. Alone. *Alone.*

Except for God.

No, that was the *really* crazy thinking. To God, if he existed, people like her were just blobs he could shove around and manipulate. Or stomp on.

She determinedly scoffed at the aloneness. She wasn't *alone.* She could talk to Mrs. L., who was always full of helpful common sense. She could even talk to Evan, who, being at a distance from the situation, might have a more objective perspective on it.

Or she could substitute action for talk, action that could force everything into the open.

Nineteen

She couldn't get away from the house for several days. Her abraded knees and bruises made walking uncomfortable. Redding's sizzling heat had followed them to the mountains. And Jace always seemed to have her under observation.

He cloaked the surveillance in solicitous concern. He called after breakfast to ask how she was feeling. He dashed over on his lunch hour to bring her a Christian novel. He called again before dinner. But before he could suggest coming over later, she said she had to spend the evening on the computer answering letters from her mother's fans.

The following afternoon, on his way to take the boys back to the river for a cooling dip, he stopped in and invited her to come along. When she said no, he lightly grumbled, "For a woman who says she's falling in love, you suddenly seem awfully busy. What comes next, that old cliché 'Sorry, I have to wash my hair tonight'?"

She skirted both the falling-in-love comment and the crack about hair washing. "I still feel a little achy."

"Sure. I understand." Now he sounded remorseful, guilty for complaining. "I'm still kicking myself for everything that happened on the Redding trip."

He leaned forward as if he wanted to kiss her, and she wanted his kiss. She wanted to fling herself into his arms and feel secure and cherished and safe. She didn't want to think what she was thinking, that a noisy, crowded river outing would be an ideal place for a never-to-be-detected "accident." She didn't want to think that cold-blooded self-protection about what she might do or what she might remember could be the motive behind his show of solicitous concern.

This was *Jace*, she reminded herself. Jace looking at her with affection and caring, Jace with no phony airs or pretenses. His denim shirt with the sleeves hacked off at the shoulders hung open above equally disreputable looking jeans. His straw hat slanted at a jaunty angle across his forehead, and his smile was so sweetly devastating that her heart did foolish things. One explosive burst of temper didn't make him a murderer!

Yet the iron trap of suspicion wouldn't release her, and she simply said stiffly, "Well, have fun."

He waved from the pickup as he followed the boys into the rutted lane through the trees, and she waved back. Yet even as she waved, that aloneness, that empty feeling of nowhere to turn for help or reassurance, invaded her again.

She thought about taking her suspicions to Mrs. L., but the housekeeper still wasn't feeling up to par, "a touch of summer blahs," she called it disparagingly, and Katy didn't want to upset her further with these wild speculations. Because they *were* wild. And irrational and incredible. She should simply bury them and forget any thought that she might not be the real Kat "Katy" Cavanaugh.

"Why don't you take some time off?" Katy suggested to Mrs. L. at breakfast the next day, concerned because the housekeeper's puffy eyes looked as if they'd barely closed all night. "How long has it been since you've had a vacation? You could go visit Evan."

"No, no, I belong here. I'll be fine. And you need someone here to look after you," the housekeeper scolded lightly. "Every time you get out of my sight something disastrous seems to happen to you."

True, Katy thought ruefully. But she didn't abandon her plan.

~ ~ ~ ~ ~

Two mornings later, with the predicted temperature for the day down a few degrees, she slipped out of bed before Mrs. L. was up, packed a lunch and a plastic bottle of water in the backpack, and left a note saying she was going for a hike. She carefully didn't say where she was going, but she added a cheery PS: *Don't worry, I'll stay away from the river, and I won't get lost. I'm taking a compass.*

She'd found the compass in her father's workshop. She had no idea how to make practical use of it, but perhaps it would reassure Mrs. L. that she knew what she was doing. Not being in a panic this time, she figured she could find her way simply by being careful.

She was also, although she didn't mention it in the note, carrying a short-handled shovel.

She had already decided she could eliminate the woods to the right of the meadow, the area Jace and the boys crossed when going to the river. She'd found the necklace to the left of the meadow, so that was most likely where the body, if there was a body, was buried.

She entered the woods approximately where she'd come out the other time, pausing briefly to glance back at the school. Jace was undoubtedly up, but he surely wouldn't be watching her this early in the morning, would he? Of course not. She'd never so much as hinted to him that she might try to search the woods. Yet she couldn't escape the feeling that he'd been keeping track of her the last few days. Joe had been over too, bringing Mrs. L. a box of candy he'd gotten for her in Redding and staying longer than usual to watch TV with her on the small kitchen set.

She shook off the someone-is-watching feeling and plunged into the thick woods. Her first thought had been simply to locate the spot where she'd found the necklace, but on reflection she'd realized she needed to expand the search. The necklace could have been torn off when the murderer set the body down while he dug a hole, but it also could have been lost while the body was being carried through the woods.

She started with a brisk sense of organization and efficiency. She would head toward the river, staying parallel with the meadow. At the river—well, not quite to the river, she decided with a shudder, surely no need to go that far—she would turn and work her way back. With that system she could search the entire woods in an orderly series of back and forth sweeps.

She pushed determinedly through the trees and brush, eyes prowling all sides for any sign of a mound or depression, anything out of the ordinary that might indicate the ground had been disturbed at some time.

If the purpose of this excursion into the woods were not so gruesome, she would have enjoyed it. The shade was cool even though summer heat had dried the leaves and needles to a crackle underfoot. There was the bright flash of a bluejay, the chatter of a squirrel, nature slowly sculpting a ragged stump into a silvery work of art. Moss covered a shaded upthrust of rock in green velvet. A pile of fresh sawdust at the end of an old log puzzled her until she saw ants carrying out a speck at a time as they industriously excavated the interior. A faintly mysterious though not unpleasant scent of the endless process of fallen leaves and needles changing to become one with the earth beneath. On a practical basis, she was better dressed this time, in long pants and lightweight-but-long-sleeved shirt, so she didn't get scratched every time she moved.

Keeping to a set distance from the meadow was not easy. The heavy brush and uneven ground combined to force her into a zigzag course, but the compass did, at least, keep her from going in circles. When she was close enough to the river that the rush of rapids prickled her skin, she made a ninety-degree turn, followed that course for what she thought was another hundred feet, and started back the direction she had come.

Here, deeper in the woods, the going got rougher, her plan for methodical search further sabotaged by natural obstacles. Rocks, some small enough to get into her shoes, others large enough to force detour. Brush, sometimes so dense she had to use the shovel to batter her way through it. Blackberry vines slyly creeping under clothes and snagging her skin. A slither of sinuous movement at her feet potently reminding her to watch her step for snakes. She tumbled into a shallow basin concealed by brush and lay there, breathing shallowly as she listened to the small creaks and rustles and squeaks of the forest. Or maybe they weren't all innocent sounds of the forest! She looked over her shoulder, half expecting to see a face staring at her through the tangled branches.

Get a grip, she told herself fiercely. *This is just a sunny day in the woods, not the Twilight Zone.*

She crawled out of the basin and struggled on. Once she came on a spot she thought could be where she'd found the necklace, though now the gooey mud was dried to a mosaic of cracks curling at the edges. Nearby a suspicious looking mound made her heart pound, but a cautious probe with the shovel revealed it was only the long-decayed remains of some fallen log.

Doggedly she kept on. She found another spot of dried mud, and it, too, could have been where she'd found the necklace. She ate her lunch, rested, and struggled on. A doe and fawn jumped up almost at her feet, their liquid, startled eyes momentarily meeting her equally startled gaze. She was in rough hills now, always going up or down, perhaps even off her own property. Once she fought her way up to an exposed outcropping of rock, thinking she could better orient herself if she could see the house or school. But all she saw was more forest, the treetops below her bird-perch viewpoint thick and green and spiky, the sharp outlines lost as the forest rolled in mountain waves to soft blue silhouettes in the distance.

The aloneness hit her again. She could plunge off this rock, tumble into some hidden niche beneath the treetops, and be lost forever.

The foolish futility of all this struck her then, and she almost laughed at the insolence of this search. Did she think she could rush out like some child looking for Easter eggs and instantly uncover incriminating evidence to expose a killer? There could be a dozen bodies buried out here, even a hundred, and she'd never find them.

She gave it up then. Using the compass, she thought she was headed directly for the house, but hours later she found herself still several miles away from it on the road she and Mrs. L. had taken on their ill-fated excursion into the mountains. The sun had set by the time she dragged into the driveway. Jace's pickup spun up beside her before she reached the door.

"Katy, where have you been? I called, and Mrs. L. told me you weren't back from a hike yet!" He looked both concerned and angry. "What were you *doing?*"

Looking for a body. Finding a body would have proved murder. But *not* finding one didn't prove it did not exist.

He eyed the shovel. "You were *digging?*"

She'd almost forgotten she was carrying the shovel. It seemed like an attached extension of her weary arm now. "I thought maybe there could be Indian artifacts or something. Arrowheads."

It was a limp excuse, and they both knew it, but all he said was, "Then I hope you didn't find any, because digging them up is illegal."

Inside, he started to jump on Mrs. L. for not calling him earlier, but Katy cut him off. "Everything turned out fine, so no need to make a federal case out of it, okay? I just want something to eat, a bath, and a good night's sleep."

She did sleep, but she woke early, already restless. She padded barefoot to the living room and stared across the road at the Damascus dormitory. Jace was in there somewhere. Jace, sweet, caring, in love with her, wanting to share his Lord with her? Or Jace, wily, deceptive, dangerous murderer hiding behind noble dedication to Christian deeds?

Maybe what she needed was to get away from here, she thought suddenly. Go off somewhere to think and wait out her memory return.

Was this tenuous, confused feeling the way she had felt, if she *was* Kat Cavanaugh, months ago when she left the ranch? Had she fled because she was frightened and uncertain then, too?

But if she went away now, where would she go? Back to New York to revive her career? Perhaps she could do it and still avoid Barry.

No, she didn't want to be any closer to Barry than she was right now!

Twenty

"Barry!"

He turned from an observation of Mt. Shasta when she opened the door. He smiled as confidently as if he were arriving with an engraved invitation in hand. "Hi, Kat."

His white shorts and open-throated, white cotton shirt looked cool and crisp in spite of the heat, as if he were ready to step onto the tennis courts of some expensive country club. Katy didn't invite him in even though he squinted at her through a blinding blaze of sun.

"What are you doing here?"

"Is that any way to greet your fiancé?" he chided.

"You're not my fiancé!"

He tilted his head as if considering disputing that but opted for another winning smile instead. "I still want to be."

She remembered what her former roommate had said about his professional problems. "The agency is in trouble so you're coming on bended knee to…?"

"Kat," he said reproachfully.

"Katy!" she corrected sharply, even as she felt a twinge of guilt for her rudeness.

"Your memory is still incomplete?"

She considered the delicately phrased question, wary about revealing any more to him about the shadows in her head than she had already unwisely done. Had he come to probe her brain to see what dangerous possibilities lurked there? Or to make sure she didn't live long enough to remember she wasn't Kat Cavanaugh? Or was he quite innocent, believing she really

225

was Kat and here simply for the reason he stated, to win her back?

Alone, she thought in dismay as her thoughts wavered like some out-of-kilter scale. Alone with her suspicions of everyone.

She finally answered the question obliquely. "I still don't remember you."

"Then let's do a better job of what we didn't do very well the last time I was here, getting reacquainted." He lifted his hands appealingly. "Can't I come in? I think this deck is melting the soles of my shoes."

Reluctantly she stood back to let him enter. Mrs. L. peered out from the kitchen to see who the visitor was. An indecipherable flurry of emotions chased across her face, always tired-looking these days, but she ducked back into the kitchen without speaking.

Katy sat on the white leather sofa. She tucked her legs under her in a position that forced Barry, if he wanted to talk to her, to sit across from, not beside her. She finally tossed a neutral question into the awkward silence. "Have you seen any of my former roommates lately?"

"I heard Stephanie was leaving modeling to get married to a dentist and moving to New Jersey. She'll probably be bored to tears there, but at least she'll have good teeth." He came up with more gossip, and even though Katy couldn't help but laugh at the tartly amusing anecdotes, her tension and wariness remained on red alert.

After an hour or so, Mrs. L. came to the doorway with a frowning, I-need-to-talk-to-you look on her face. Katy excused herself and followed Mrs. L. to the kitchen.

"What's he doing here?" Mrs. L. demanded in a whisper. "How long is he staying?"

"I don't know. To both questions," Katy whispered back.

"I think you should get rid of him!"

The urgency of Mrs. L.'s whisper surprised Katy. "But I thought you liked him. The other time he was here, you even thought my going back to New York with him was a good idea."

Mrs. L. shook her head. "He's too smooth, too polished. Like glass pretending to be a diamond."

Katy trusted Mrs. L.'s instincts. They also matched her own. She'd felt much safer when Barry was three thousand miles away in New York.

And yet, if they were both wrong about Barry, if it was Jace she really had to fear, she could be safer with Barry here.

When she returned to the sofa, Barry gave a theatrical sigh and slapped his palms against his thighs. "You were discussing me, weren't you? And you're going to make me drive all the way back to Yreka to get a motel for the night."

Her decision came impulsively. "No, you can stay here."

Immediately, as if afraid she might change her mind, he ran out to get his suitcase. They had a pleasant dinner, although Mrs. L. served it with considerably less than her usual hospitality.

"What's the matter with her?" Barry whispered as she whisked away his plate without giving him a chance for seconds on the baked chicken. "She acts as if she thinks I might take an ax to both of you in your beds."

Katy assumed the comment was meant to be humorous, but she was too tense to be amused. Especially on this subject. "She hasn't been feeling well lately."

The phone rang just after they'd finished the peach shortcake. Katy suggested Barry take his coffee to the living room, and she answered the phone in the kitchen, out of his presence.

"I was thinking we might take a drive up in the mountains this evening, but I see a car in your driveway." Jace was obviously fishing for information. Acting like a jealous boyfriend? Or something darker and more dangerous?

"Barry's here."

"Were you expecting him?" Jace sounded surprised.

"No."

"What does he want?"

She hesitated. "I'm not sure."

"I'll come over and run him off, if you'd like."

The half-teasing, half-serious offer should have made her feel better, but all it did was send her throat muscles into a spasm, as if a web were tightening around her neck. Who could she trust?

"I'll keep that in mind," she finally managed to say lightly.

"I love you, Katy," he said huskily. "Keep that in mind, too."

Do you? Or was this just another cog in the wheel of some deadly plan?

"And the Lord loves you too. You can call on either of us, both of us, whenever you're in need. You have my phone number, and you don't need one to get to God."

She hung up without saying good-bye, half angry. His gullible boys might fall for that glib phone-number bit about God, but she didn't.

In spite of Barry's attempt to be charismatic and entertaining, the evening plummeted downhill. Several times, even as he smiled, Katy saw anger flash in his eyes when she avoided his touch and failed to respond to his determined efforts to charm her. Finally, at what she suspected was much earlier than a New York bedtime, he headed for the stairs.

With a foot on the bottom rung he turned and asked, "Is there someone else, Kat?"

She automatically started to correct the name, then let it go. There was something so nearly wistful about the question that she couldn't be heartlessly rude. "Yes, there is," she admitted honestly. She hesitated, on the brink of pouring out all her doubts and fears about Jace and her own identity.

"The religious fanatic from across the road?" Barry's sudden smile was more like a sneer. "I guess I'm not surprised. Even before you disappeared, I figured you had the hots for him."

He turned his back on her, and Katy could only gasp at the crude statement and how wrong she had been in judging him "wistful." And how close she had come to making another mistake in confiding in him.

For the first time ever, she carefully locked her bedroom door.

She fell into a restless, sheet-twisting sleep. After an hour, she woke and instantly jumped up to check the door. The room felt airless and stuffy, but she didn't want to risk the vulnerability of an open window. Barry's coarse comment still prickled her skin like a slimy caress. She paced around the bed, avoiding the stain on the carpet even though she couldn't see it in the dark. Mrs. L. had tried again to get it out, and the wine blood color was less intense now, but the stain, as if it were insidiously stalking her, had spread to cover a larger area. Again it made her ask, had Jace lied to her about that night?

She went back to bed. Woke again. The hands of the clock glowed on 2:30 A.M. The pit of the night. Sunset long gone, sunrise only a distant hope. She lay there rigidly, wondering if something specific had wakened her. The giveaway creak in the hallway outside her door? A hand stealthily seeking the doorknob? She listened for long, taut moments, but no sounds came. A light flared at her window. Fire? A forest ranger had stopped by the other day, warning that the woods were tinder dry now.

She yanked the drapes open, almost expecting to see flames

crackling in the trees, but the light was only a car on the road, its headlights flashing against her window as if it had briefly angled toward the driveway before speeding on by. One of the marijuana "farmers" Mrs. L. claimed lived hidden in the mountains? A drug agent after them?

She left the drape open after the taillights disappeared, feeling less closed-in with a dim glow of starlight filtering into the room. She returned to bed but didn't lie down. Instead she clasped her arms around her bent legs and rested her head on her knees. A shiver rippled through her. Why should she shiver? The room wasn't cold.

She shivered again. Methodically, more to distract herself than anything, she analyzed the cause. Apprehension? Nerves? Fear? Yes, to all. Fear of what? Barry. Jace. That she was Kat Cavanaugh. That she *wasn't* Kat Cavanaugh. That her memory might never return. That her memory *would* return.

And then she knew she was dodging the real issue, because the shiver was above all a desperate cry of inescapable *aloneness.*

Alone. Alone. *Alone.* She tried to halt the relentless parade of words, but the drumbeat marched on. Alone. Alone.

No. Not alone.

The denial came with an unshakable serenity. She was uncertain from where the words came, inside or outside her, but she skeptically defied them. *Oh?*

Never alone.

She flicked the switch on the lamp and reluctantly reached for the Bible on the floor, where she'd scornfully tossed it one night.

Okay, Lord, if you're there, show me I'm not alone, she challenged.

Her fingers rippled the pages as if guided by some unerring force in her subconscious. Deuteronomy. Her forefinger raced back and forth across the lines like some wild animal dashing for the security of its lair. Chapter 33. Her eyes jumped ahead of her finger as if they knew exactly where to look. Verse 27. *The eternal God is your refuge, and underneath are the everlasting arms.*

The everlasting arms. Holding her. Protecting her. Giving her refuge. Not just for this life but for all eternity.

She held the book to her chest. Was that true?

She closed her eyes, looking inward. If she accepted this, would the dark pit in her mind open to reveal her past and who she was and why she knew where to look for these words? She waited, but not even a shadow stirred. Yet from somewhere came guidance to a sweet Psalm. *God is our refuge and strength, an ever present help in trouble.*

A promise added to the vow of Deuteronomy, that he was not only refuge but strength. And with a broken-dam acknowledgment of her own utter helplessness, her own barren aloneness, she finally let herself enter that refuge and lean on that strength, draw from it, let it fill body and spirit like a life-giving transfusion. She roamed other verses, each one an inexplicable combination of the wonderfully fresh and new, yet also familiar, as if she were walking into rooms she had known and loved before. Coming home.

Home. She let the Bible rest against her knees and stared off into space. Home. Because she'd been here before.

Not here in this house, but here in this home place of the heart and spirit. With Jesus as her Savior and Lord. With his eternal Word as her foundation and life guide.

She knew this, yet she had turned her back on him, rejected and abandoned him. And resentfully thought he had abandoned and forgotten her, too. Her fingers flew through the Bible again, the order of the books like rungs on a familiar stairway. Proverbs, Ecclesiastes, Song of Songs, yes, there it was, *Isaiah.*

Oh, yes, Isaiah 49! *But Zion said, "The LORD has forsaken me, the Lord has forgotten me." "Can a mother forget the baby at her breast and have no compassion on the child she has borne? Though she may forget, I will not forget you!"*

Yes, she had forgotten him. Why? Why? Had she forgotten *everything* in some rebellious determination to forget and thrust him out of her life? Or did the Lord have to take her memory away in order to bring her back to him because she had earlier rejected him? Because, no matter what she accused, he had never forgotten her! He had faithfully led her full circle, back into the security of his love. Jace had said it that first time she went to the river with him and the boys. *He doesn't give up on us even if we give up on him. He's working in our lives whether or not we recognize it at the time.*

Jace.

Jace the believer or Jace the deceiver?

At this moment not even Jace and the conflicts between her love and suspicion of him mattered because words from the Psalms, like a circling dove, gently floated down to rest on her soul.

Be still and know that I am God.

And Katy was still and knew that he was God, and she was alone no more.

She woke and, as always, immediately peered hopefully within her mind. No change. The dark pit was as closed and sealed as always. But *she* was changed, wonderfully new, gloriously different! She sat up and stretched.

Different in her body, aware that the lifeblood coursing through her upraised arms and outstretched legs was a sweet gift from God. That sight of sunlight streaming through the window and dust motes dancing in its beam, that sound of songbirds trilling outside the window and the raucous squawk of crows circling the garden were also his gifts.

Different in her heart, anger and rebellion and resentment toward the Lord melted away. Glorious knowledge that Jesus was her Savior and she had come home to him.

Home.

Even in her joy, this morning that word sent questions rippling through her. Because these changes *were* a coming home; she knew it. She wasn't coming to the Lord for the very first time. So what did that mean? She knew from her actions and the life she'd lived that she had not been a believer before she disappeared from the ranch. Had she made a decision for Christ, then resentfully abandoned it for some unknown reason, all in the space of those few months before Mrs. L. identified her at a hospital in Oregon?

But those questions, of course, assumed she was Katy Cavanaugh.

And if she wasn't Katy, if crickets and computers and a nagging feeling of something undone came from another life, another past...

A tap on the door startled her. Barry? An instant fight-or-flight jolt of adrenaline made her grab the lamp as a weapon. Then she relaxed. *Not alone. Never alone.* "Yes?" she said, her tone normal.

"Sweetie, are you okay?" Mrs. L. sounded anxious.

Katy picked up the clock. Almost nine-thirty! She never slept this late. No wonder Mrs. L. was concerned. Now she could smell the tantalizing aroma of cinnamon rolls and coffee. "I'm getting up right now." She swung her legs to the floor. "Is Barry up yet?"

"He's gone."

"Gone where?"

"I don't know. The car was gone when I got up. I thought perhaps he just went out for an early drive, but I peeked in his room, and all his things are gone too."

Katy hastily showered and dressed in shorts and a tank top. In spite of brilliant sunshine on the bedroom side of the house, the breakfast-nook window revealed swollen clouds over the mountains in the opposite direction, as if building toward a thunderstorm later in the day.

"He didn't leave a note?" Katy asked as Mrs. L. placed scrambled eggs and a fragrant, plate-sized cinnamon roll in front of her.

"No, but good riddance, I'd say." Mrs. L. dismissed Barry with a righteous sniff and untied her apron. "I'm more worried about Maggie. I haven't seen her since yesterday afternoon. I'm going out to look for her. Once before she got caught in a tree, and Joe had to rescue her."

"I'll come help."

"No, no, you finish your breakfast." She patted Katy's shoulder. "I'm probably fussing over nothing. But you know how much those silly cats mean to me."

Katy finished the roll and helped herself to half of another and more coffee. She wasn't overly concerned about Maggie. The cats led a busy life roaming their territory, and the big orange cat was probably just curled up somewhere sleeping off a night of heavy mouse hunting.

She pinched off pieces of the roll, absentmindedly savoring the rich cinnamon taste as she considered Barry's unexpected departure. She was relieved that he had left without making some unpleasant scene, but she was vaguely uneasy anyway. Had he really gone home to New York, or was he up to something devious?

Yet she couldn't devote much energy even to that disturbing

question. She was too full of this joyous homecoming of the heart, the glorious knowledge that Christ had loved her before, that he'd loved her through whatever had driven her away from him, that he loved her still and always would. He'd gone to the cross for her!

She brought the Bible from her bedroom and, over another cup of coffee, browsed the pages with more satisfaction than if she were in some enormous mall with treasures free for the taking. Because what material treasures could compare with these nuggets of wisdom and enlightenment, these promises of love and salvation?

She was deep in Luke: *Are not five sparrows sold for two pennies? Yet not one of them is forgotten by God.* She was pleasurably lost in those words, reminding her again that she had never been forgotten, when shouts penetrated her consciousness. Mrs. L. ran through the back door.

"Katy, Katy, I've been yelling and screaming!"

Katy jumped up, alarmed by Mrs. L's frantic panting and crimson face. "Calm down! What's wrong?"

The housekeeper patted her chest as if her pounding heart threatened to burst through her rib cage. "It's Maggie! She's stranded up in a tree and too scared to come down." Mrs. L. ran out of breath and sagged against the kitchen counter. "Oh, Katy, the branch is right next to the river, and I'm so afraid she's going to fall in and drown!"

Katy stopped short in the act of slipping on her shoes, her instant readiness to help rescue Maggie sabotaged by this revelation. The river? Mrs. L. wanted her to confront the *river*?

She offered an alternate idea. "I'll call Jace, and he or Joe can—"

"No, it'll take too long to get them over here! Just come, Katy, please! I can almost reach her on the branch but not

235

quite. But you're taller, and you can save her. Please, Katy!" Tears and sweat streamed down Mrs. L.'s red face. She must have run all the way!

Katy hesitated a moment longer. Not the river, anywhere but the river! Then she gritted her teeth determinedly. She loved that silly cat too, and she wasn't going to let her fear cost it its life. "Okay. I'll get the car out of the garage"

"The car?" Mrs. L. looked startled. "But there's no road back to where she's at."

"The meadow is so dry the ground is hard enough to drive on now, and it'll be faster than running. And you're in no condition to run back to the river anyway!"

Katy grabbed the car keys off the hook, flung the garage door open and backed the car out. Mrs. L. still seemed hesitant about taking the car, but she climbed in when Katy pushed the door open. She clutched the seat as Katy raced the little red convertible across the meadow, grass scraping the underside. Clouds covered a third of the sky now, the air thick and muggy. They got almost to the line of trees before a rear tire bogged down in a lingering soft spot.

Katy didn't waste time fighting the spinning tire. She flung the door open and jumped out. "Where?"

Mrs. L. pointed to a spot downstream from where the ground had crumbled beneath Katy that day. Determinedly she willed herself to ignore the roar of the rapids, the crashing white water, and the panic in her heart. *Not alone!* She pushed her way through the brush, the older and shorter-legged Mrs. L. trailing behind her.

"I can't see her!" Katy yelled. But she couldn't avoid seeing the river. The drying heat of summer had lowered the water level, and not so much raw power surged through this narrow spot, but it looked more treacherous than ever, with dark rocks exposed like the teeth of an evil grin. "Maybe she got down by herself—"

Mrs. L. caught up with her, puffing and red faced again. "No, she's right there on that branch closest to the water! Can't you see her? Oh, Katy, please get her before she falls!"

Katy edged closer to the water's edge, eyes searching the thick foliage overhead for some flash of orange fur. Thankfully, the ground beneath her feet here was a solid rock ledge a couple of feet above the water, no danger of crumbling. If she could just keep her eyes away from the dizzying cauldron of surging, bucking white water, leaping as if greedily reaching to snatch her from the ledge—

No, water has no consciousness, she reminded herself fiercely. *Don't panic! You'll be okay if you don't panic.* "Maggie?" she called hopefully. "Here, kitty, kitty—"

From behind a barrier of brush he watched her searching for a nonexistent cat in the branches over her head. He neither stiffened nor hunkered down in the brush when she frantically glanced his direction. He knew his camouflage cap and clothing and the daubs of dirt on his face blended perfectly into the background, that she wouldn't see him even if she looked straight at him. He almost smiled with the thrill of victory. Just a few moments more.

But she wasn't quite close enough to the edge of the ledge yet.

Just a couple more steps, *he commanded her silently. He hoped the thunderstorm would break soon. A pounding rain would erase any tracks. Not that anyone should be looking for incriminating tracks anyway. This would be just a tragic accident. That's it, he crooned silently as she edged closer to the brink of the ledge. Another step…*

His hand tightened around the dead branch he'd swung against a tree and broken to a suitable length. She stopped, and he cursed softly under his breath. If she turned back too soon…

Do it now.

Swiftly, delicately, like slipping a slender key in a keyhole, he threaded the long branch through the brush, positioned it just behind her shoulder blades.

And shoved.

Twenty - One

Katy screamed as a force like a battering ram punched her between the shoulder blades. She plunged forward, hand ripped from the branch she clutched for balance. Arms outflung, for one endless moment she hung spread-eagle over the churning water below. And then it rushed up and smashed into her like a sheet of steel before treacherously melting away and closing over her. The primitive force sucked her under and battered her blindly against underwater obstacles, whirling and tossing her like some demonic machine on mad rampage, tearing at her lungs, contorting her body.

It shot her upwards, and her bursting chest instinctively grabbed a lungful of air before she was dragged under again, spinning like some helpless bug going down a deadly drain. Burying her in a liquid netherworld without light or air, where there was only terror filling every nerve, every muscle, every cell. *Lord, help me!*

Yet with the terror and the plea for help, deep within her mind an explosion beyond the physical detonated, a blaze of illumination that lit up the dark pit and split its walls like the bursting of a bubble. Out poured terror-memory of another time like this, falling, whirling in a chaos of white water.

The river flung her against something hard and unyielding. She fought to escape, water pressing her against the obstacle with lung-crushing force, raw instinct flinging all thoughts of anything but survival out of her mind. She clawed upwards, fingers and elbows, knees, toes, every inch of her body battling for survival.

Her head pushed through the surface, and she gasped and choked, but she was breathing, *breathing* as the water surged around her. A slosh filled her mouth, and she struggled for another inch or two to escape the strangling clutch of the river and the barrier trapping her.

She shook her head, realization dimly coming that the rock she was crushed against was not an enemy but a tiny island of safety. She clamped her legs around it and risked one hand to swipe water from her eyes and clear her blurred vision.

And then vision inside her also came unblurred as a flood-burst of memories streamed through the shattered walls of the dark pit. So many memories they overwhelmed her! A life passing before her eyes, but not Kat Cavanaugh's life! The shadows were no longer faceless silhouettes. It was all there. Joy and sadness, love and loss, computers and—oh, Cricket! For an instant the old pain was so great that it even submerged the desperate fear of the moment.

Then the current dragged her to one side, and she fought to regain her precarious position centered on the rock protruding from the water. Cautiously she turned her head, and astonished relief charged through her. She was no more than eight or nine feet from shore, a bare three armstrokes from the ledge! Safety! The river had taken her on a savage carousel ride more vertical and circular than horizontal.

The giddy relief vanished as desolate realization set in. She might be only three armstrokes from the ledge, but safety was as unreachable as the treetops looming above the river. If she let go, water swooping in slick green torrents past both sides of the rock would instantly plunge her into the lethal ambush of rocks and savage white water below.

Yet she couldn't hold on long. The cold water was already stealing the feeling from her legs. But where was Mrs. L.?

"Mrs. L.! I'm here, down here!" she shouted, the words ending in a sputtering gurgle as she slipped on the slick rock and her mouth plunged beneath the surface.

Desperately she fought to regain her few inches of sanctuary on the slippery rock. Was the older woman, already exhausted from running back to the house once, frantically racing for help again? Or was she battling her way downstream, trying to find Katy among the rocks in that maelstrom?

If she could just get far enough up on the rock to keep from losing consciousness before help came....

Out of the corner of her eye she saw movement on the ledge. Then Mrs. L.'s familiar face peered down at her. Seen from Katy's position at water level, the housekeeper's stocky, matronly body looked abnormally tall and gaunt looming against the cloud-covered sky, her face uncharacteristically long and somber.

"Keys in the car!" Katy gasped as Mrs. L. just stood there. "Get help!"

Mrs. L.'s only movement was to clutch her hands together helplessly, her face twisted as if in pain. Another figure appeared beside her. In spite of the camouflage clothes and dirt-daubed face, Katy recognized him from the photographs. Evan! Evan miraculously dropped out of nowhere to save her!

She waved one arm frantically because it almost seemed as if he didn't see her, the way he just stood there with arms folded. "Evan! Down here, here!"

He dropped to a sitting position on the ledge and dangled his legs over the edge like some tourist idly surveying a view. Katy didn't understand. Why did he just sit there watching her as if she were some bit of driftwood caught on a rock?

"I'm sorry, Katy, so very sorry." Tears ran down Mrs. L.'s face, still pink from exertion, and she swiped a knuckle across her cheek. "I didn't want to do it, but there wasn't any other way." She gave her son a sideways, half-hopeful glance.

Until that moment raw survival instinct hadn't given Katy time to think how she'd tumbled into the water. Now, it almost seemed as if she'd been *pushed*. But that couldn't be!

She watched mother and son, unmoving as paper cutouts as they watched her desperately clinging to the rock, and she knew the truth.

Yes. Pushed.

She clawed a fraction of an inch higher on the rock, found a toehold for one foot. They weren't going to rescue her.

Not Evan, muscular and well built, good looking in spite of the mud-daubed face and camouflage visor cap pulled low over his eyes. Evan, who'd pretended to share his memories with her, had made her laugh with stories of childhood escapades. Not Mrs. L., who'd doctored her scratches and baked cinnamon rolls for her and given her a crash course in Kat Cavanaugh 101.

A flood of visions tumbled chaotically in her head, the real past mixing with the past she'd tried to learn and assimilate and make her own.

"I'm not the real Kat. We both know that now, don't we?"

Anguished look from Mrs. L., indifference from Evan. He swung his legs and pulled the cap a little lower.

"You killed her, didn't you, Evan?" Katy asked. "The real Kat."

How very strange, Katy thought with detached numbness as she slipped and then laboriously regained the inch she'd lost on her precarious island of safety. Here she was, carrying on an almost polite conversation with the man who had killed her predecessor and was in the process of murdering her to keep that first crime from surfacing. The river still roared, but the sound seemed muted now, as if their ears filtered it out to let only the voices through.

Mrs. L. put a hand to her mouth as if in sudden horror or

astonishment, but any surprise she felt, Katy knew, was only surprise that Katy now knew this truth about the real Kat's death, not that Mrs. L. had just been hit with a shocking new fact. Mrs. L. had known all along that the real Kat was dead and that Evan had killed her. Had known when she made false identification in an Oregon hospital. Had known when she cheerfully handed over the real Kat's life and career and material assets to a stranger. Anything for Evan.

Oh, she was good, Katy thought with a detached observation even as she swallowed a sudden slap of water in the face. Very sweet-little-lady believable. Making up that oh-so-credible story about taking Kat to meet friends in Redding. Glibly dovetailing the dangerous awkwardness of a Katy with a different personality into the little-girl Kat of long ago, instantly inventing on-the-spot explanations about those Fourth-of-July shadows in Katy's head and any other discrepancies that arose, giving today's truly dramatic lost-cat performance.

"Maggie's fine, isn't she? Where is she? Safely locked in your bedroom?" Katy asked, and, as if now welded to the truth, Mrs. L. nodded guiltily.

"And there wasn't any Aunt Cora desperately needing a transplant, was there? Evan got the money." Just as Joe had suspected.

Mrs. L. didn't answer those questions, just gave her son an uneasy side-glance.

A sudden twitch of current swept Katy's legs into the deadly flow, and she laboriously dragged them back to the rock again. How long could she hold out here? Not as long as mother and cold-blooded son could. No wonder Mrs. L. had been so tired and upset lately. She knew this was coming, and she hadn't wanted to do it, yet some cross-wired sense of protective mother love forced her to it.

"You somehow managed to run Barry out this morning,

didn't you?" Katy said to her. "Because his being here would have ruined all your plans."

Again, Mrs. L. could only say, "I'm so sorry, Katy." As if, even though she knew this wasn't the real Kat in the water, the substitute she'd chosen had become a "Katy" in her mind.

The chill of the water was seeping into Katy's muscles and bones now. Hypothermia, wasn't it? But that wouldn't get her. She'd drown first. Mrs. L. leaned forward, still crying, and started to say something, but Evan flung out an arm to stop her.

"Don't talk to her. She's just stalling for time."

It was a command and warning with such weird logic that hysterical laughter simmered on the perimeter of Katy's fear. As if *conversation* were some valid delaying tactic that could turn away the river's deadly power and give her a chance at survival!

"Why did you kill her, Evan?" Even as she asked the question, other thoughts made his answer irrelevant. *Jace, oh, Jace!* How unfairly suspicious of him she'd been! Her body and limbs were almost beyond feeling, but inside, her heart could still ache. She'd never get to tell him that no daunting list separated them, that she loved him, that the faith he lived by was her faith too. And Barry. She'd also been unfair to him! Whatever his faults, he was no murderer. And unjust to Joe, too, suspecting sweet old Joe of deliberately trying to run over her.

Evan stood up and with unexpected fury hurled a handful of high-water debris stranded on the ledge at her. "Shut up!"

The photographs hadn't shown how short he was, she realized. Muscular and well built but barely an inch or two taller than his mother. Once she had innocently thought that if anyone could release her memory from the dark pit, it would be Evan. And he had! But the irony that it should be like *this*, while trying to murder her. A found memory, a lost life. The river trash bobbed briefly within inches of her face, then swept down the deadly green slide to the churning death trap beyond. She heard the first rumbles of thunder, and raindrops dimpled the slick swoop of water beside her.

Suddenly Mrs. L. grabbed Evan's arm and shook it, her other hand pointing to something behind them. With their backs to her, the sound of the river and more thunder blurred their voices. Then, as suddenly as the turning on of some cosmic sprinkler, a crashing downpour dropped an instant veil between her and the ledge. Evan disappeared, and she thought he had run to escape the downpour, but he returned a moment later carrying something. A long, stout branch! Hope unexpectedly burgeoned within her. He'd changed his mind! He was going to rescue her after all!

She reached for the branch as he thrust it across the slick sweep of green water. It jabbed her shoulder, the pain sharp in spite of its slow message reaching her brain, but a little pain didn't matter. Nor did the rain battering her face, half blinding her. If she could just get hold of the branch, he could pull her to safety.

Cautiously she released the grip of one arm on the rock and tried to snag the branch. It jumped out of reach, and she stretched farther. Almost, *almost*. It wasn't until Evan moved sideways to reposition the pole, and it struck her neck that she realized the deadly truth. He wasn't trying to rescue her. He was trying to shove her off the rock, push her into the green slide to certain death!

For a strange moment time crashed to a stop. She thought of her wonderful experience coming home to the Lord last night. *Thank you, Lord, thank you for bringing me home before it was too late!* Because even if this life ended now, this wasn't all there was. Eternity waited beyond. But even with that comfort, she wasn't giving up. Not yet! She still had a little strength of her own, and she still had all the Lord's strength! If she could grab the pole, even if Evan let go, maybe it would catch crossways between rock and ledge, and she could work her way across it to shore.

"They're coming! They're almost here!" Mrs. L.'s body seemed turned to stone in the rain, only her head moving as her gaze flipped wildly from some invisible presence in the meadow to Evan and Katy, and turbulent hope flooded through Katy again. Someone was out there; someone was coming! If she could just hold on a few minutes longer.

The pole battered her, and she couldn't escape the cold-blooded blows. Head, shoulders, hands. The blows rained down on her, relentless and merciless, with a fury that eclipsed the pounding rain. And even through the growing numbness of her body, a cruel jab at her wrist brought such sharp pain that she cried out and let go of the rock. Instinctively she lunged for the only thing within reach, the pole.

She caught it, felt it buck and twist in her hands as Evan tried to wrench it away from her. Blindly she clung to it. Then it was loose, unfettered. She hadn't lost her grip, but he had! Arms windmilling wildly, feet slipping on the wet ledge.

For a peculiar moment something like a dark shadow loomed over her, arms outstretched like the wings of a vulture. A splash rolled a fresh but temporary wave over her, insignificant in the deluge of rain and river already surrounding her from above and below. Momentarily his face, terrified now, slid by only inches from hers, his hands desperately reaching for her. Then the swoop of green water took him, and her, too, sweeping her into its relentless pull.

She jolted to a stop, water beating her face, pounding her body, stretching it as if she were on some liquid rack. Desperately she tried to get her nose above the choking deluge. Dimly, through a ragged veil of surging water, she saw figures on the ledge. Two figures, no three, then one was gone. They were shouting, she thought, but the roar of the river filled her ears now. It was within her, a part of her. Her head lolled to one side. It would be so much easier just to let go, release this agonizing pain in her shoulders.

Hold on, Katy! Strangely, she had time to wonder where the command came from. From within herself? from a shouting figure? from the Lord? She hung on, not even certain what she was holding to. Only that her arms were stretched out in front of her, her hands clamped on something, legs trailing helplessly, buffeted by the current.

Yes, the long branch had caught between rock and ledge! But for what purpose? She couldn't fight her way upstream, could do nothing but cling here until her arms gave way or the branch broke.

And then she was moving! Moving forward, inch by inch moving against the relentless flow of the river. How? She went under, came up choking, but she didn't let go. Dimly she knew that even if consciousness failed her, she wouldn't let go. Because, whether in this life or the next, she held fast to the eternal hands of the Lord.

Then human hands were lifting her, dragging her across the rocky ledge, prying the rough branch from the death grip of her hands. Weakly she rolled to her stomach and then her knees, her head hanging between her outspread arms, coughing, spitting, gasping, choking, throwing up.

She felt strong arms encircle her and a body shelter her protectively from the pounding rain, heard wordless murmurs of comfort. She relaxed limply. Jace's body, Jace's murmurs. She couldn't say anything. Words couldn't get past her numbed lips. But she could think them. *Jace, Jace, I love you. And thank you, Lord, thank you for sending him to save me!*

He slipped out of his shirt, dried her face, and wrapped the damp shirt around her shoulders. Safe in his arms, head pressed against his bare chest, she felt more than heard the rumble of his words as he spoke to someone else. Joe, she thought vaguely, something about looking for Evan.

Then, his body still sheltering her, she felt him lift and carry her. Brush scraped her legs as he carried her through the strip of woods and then broke into a run. Wind and rain tore at them, treacherously shifting to attack from all sides, but Jace's stride never faltered. Then he was gently setting her on something, and she dimly realized it was the seat of the pickup, out of the wind, out of the rain.

"Jace, I—" Nausea grabbed her, and she bent forward, coughing and choking.

He got a blanket from behind the seat, wrapped it around her, and cradled her against him, gently rocking her. "Shhhh. Don't try to talk."

A soft whimper escaped her as her arms, with a sudden fierce strength of their own, wound around his body, willing him to stay close. His wet hair dripped on her, but she only tightened her arms.

"It's okay now, Katy. You're safe now," he crooned soothingly. "I love you."

Even in her sweet relief that water could no longer fill her lungs at any moment, the truth rushed back at her. "Maybe not," she whispered.

"Yes! Oh, Katy, if you knew how I felt when I saw you there in the water…"

"I'm not Katy."

Twenty - Two

K aty, you've just had a terrible shock!"
Even in her dazed, half-drowned condition she realized that he didn't believe her, that he thought she was just confused, delirious, hallucinating!

She swallowed, the movement painful, her throat threatening revolt. She wanted to talk to him, wanted to tell him everything, but it was so difficult to get words out. Her voice felt strange, raspy and alien. But she must tell him one thing.

It came out in a croak. "Jace, I'm so sorry I was suspicious of you! I love you!"

He drew back in spite of the vice grip of her arms, the look on his face surprised but guarded. As if he were dealing with someone not necessarily in full control of her mind. "Suspicious of me?"

"And it wasn't you! It was Evan; all the time it was Evan." Another coughing spell shook her, and rivulets of cold sweat ran down her already shivering body. "Evan killed Kat. He tried to kill me!"

Jace tilted his head to look at her, and she saw the troubled doubt in his hazel eyes. "Katy, I saw him trying to save you! He fell in the river trying to save you!"

"No!" Wildly she realized how close Evan's scheme had come to working. If she'd drowned, he'd have claimed he'd been trying to rescue her. He had Jace as an eyewitness to back him up! And even now Jace thought she was too confused to know what she was saying. "He pushed me in! Because he knew I was remembering I'm not Kat Cavanaugh."

"You're in no condition to talk now." Jace's words cut decisively into her outpouring, as if he wanted to stop her from making more outrageous claims. In a soothing tone that angered her even in her weakness, he added, "I'll get you to the house and then come back to help Joe and Mrs. L. look for Evan."

She tried to speak, but another coughing spell grabbed her, and she could only lean limply against him. She hadn't the strength or energy to convince him now. Weakly she whispered, "I'll be okay here."

"No, you won't. Katy, you almost drowned, you're shivering, and…"

Her strength momentarily surged. "I'm not Katy!"

He hesitated, then, and asked carefully, "If you aren't Katy, who are you?"

"My name is Sara Garrison."

He looked startled, as if he had expected more vague talk about shadows and indistinct feelings rather than such a direct, specific answer. "We'll talk about this later," he finally muttered. He slid into the pickup beside her, nudging her across the bench seat with his hip. He wheeled the vehicle in a tight circle, roaring past the forlorn little red convertible, its interior soaked and rainwater puddled on the black leather seats. By now the storm had almost passed, just a sprinkle of light raindrops still pattering the meadow grass flattened by the earlier fury of the brief summer downpour.

At the house, without asking, he carried her from the pickup to the bedroom. His bare chest felt warm and solid against her chilled body. Before he could deposit her on the bed she struggled to her feet. "I'm okay. I can manage."

He balanced her lightly with his hands on her elbows, his troubled eyes questioning her condition, both physical and mental. "I hate to leave you like this, but we might still be able to find and save Evan."

"Yes. Go find Evan."

"You get out of these wet clothes and into bed." He ran his hands up and down her chilled arms, massaging them lightly, as if to give her of his own warmth and strength. "Maybe a hot bath first."

"Jace, how did you happen to be there to rescue me?"

He hesitated, as if he didn't want to take time to explain, then hurriedly said, "Joe and I were headed for our kayaking area to pick up some equipment left behind a few days ago. I saw the convertible back there near the end of the meadow and thought that was peculiar. So we went over to investigate."

A simple, logical explanation. Yet she knew there was more to it than that. "You were there because the Lord put you there to save me from Evan."

His reaction to that statement was mixed, a nod to agree that his being where she needed help was the Lord's doing, but a narrowing of his eyes in response to the strange workings of her mind concerning Evan. She could almost read *paranoid* and *delusional* written there.

"I came home to the Lord last night, Jace," she said softly. "I've been fighting it all this time. I was bitter and angry about something that happened in my life—my other life—but last night I found my way back to Him. And when I was in the water, I was scared. But I wasn't alone."

Jace's hands moved to her upper arms, and he leaned over and kissed her lightly. "I'm glad. I've prayed for this."

"But you doubt it?" she asked, sensing an undercurrent of restraint.

"I don't know what to think," he admitted. "You almost drowned, and you're telling me so many strange things. That you're not Katy, that Evan killed Kat and tried to kill you, that you're suspicious of me…"

"No, that I *was* suspicious of you but I'm not now!"

"Okay. Look, I have to go help Joe and Mrs. L. look for Evan. When he went in, she screamed and ran off down the river as if she might jump in after him. Even if he did what you say he did…"

"I know. You'd still have to try to save him."

He nodded. "I'll be back as soon as I can." He kissed her again, then headed for the door, already at a run before he reached it. She still had his shirt, and she clutched it close to her face, taking comfort in the damp male scent of it. Absentmindedly, she realized she was barefoot. The river had snatched her shoes. She suspected it had taken more than that from Evan.

She dropped to the edge of the bed when the back door slammed behind Jace, mind full to explosion with all that had happened, both today and months ago on an isolated road in Oregon and all the years of a complete lifetime before that. The past crowded her, as if there were too much memory for the disk space of her mind. She was grateful that she now knew who she was, yet knowing came with a price, a bittersweet victory because of the pain that accompanied the knowledge.

There were also bewildering spots of almost-memories that she knew weren't hers, memories that belonged in Kat Cavanaugh's past. But she'd tried so hard to be Katy Cavanaugh that even now some of the memories almost seemed to be her own. Wonderful Thornton and Mavis Cavanaugh, loving, caring parents—

But not *her* parents, because she was Sara Garrison.

She couldn't begin to sort through everything at once. It was like a mountain of photo albums she must plow through, sorting among them to find the pictures that belonged to her.

And there, at the very peak of the mountain of snapshot memories was Cricket, her pictures glowing brightest of all. Sara's heart ached with the pain of remembering sweet, loving, lost little Cricket.

No, not lost, she contradicted fiercely, because till the very end, even in the midst of her pain, Cricket had clung tightly to her little-girl faith in Jesus.

It was two hours before Jace and Joe and Mrs. L. returned to the house. Sara met them at the back door, the burgundy velvet robe she'd thrown on to chase away the chill of the river incongruous with the summer sun now blazing outside. Jace's chest, still shirtless, looked warrior strong even though rough scratches streaked the tan, and his face was tired and grim. Dirt and river water spattered Mrs. L.'s clothes, and her gray hair hung disheveled around the haggard despair of her face. Joe held back as he followed the other two into the kitchen, as if he wasn't quite sure where he fit into this strange situation.

Jace shook his head in answer to the unspoken question in the small tilt of Sara's eyebrows. "We couldn't find him."

"Maybe he climbed out of the river somewhere?"

Jace glanced at Mrs. L., as if he hated to deprive her of hope, but his answer was decisive. "No. The river didn't let him escape."

Even now, Sara couldn't feel hatred for Evan, just a bewildered horror. And an aching for Mrs. L.'s pain, even though Mrs. L. had aided Evan in his murderous scheme. She glanced between Jace and Mrs. L., who had slumped to a bench in the breakfast nook. Mrs. L.'s face, crumpled with grief, also held a dazed disbelief, as if she couldn't quite believe it had really come to this.

"Did she tell you anything?"

"Yes. That Evan was in love with Kat and had been for a long time. He stayed on here at the ranch after Barry left, thinking he had a chance with her after she'd broken her engagement to Barry. But when she laughed at him and made fun of his height and said she wouldn't even be seen in public with such a shrimp, much less consider marrying him, he snapped."

Mrs. L. visibly cringed, although whether from horror at what her son had done or from hearing again the deliberate cruelty of Kat's scornful words to him, Sara didn't know. The housekeeper's eyes remained on her hands, her expression so hopeless that even after knowing she had lured Sara to the river for her death, Sara still felt a ragged sympathy and compassion for this woman who had been so good to her in so many ways.

"So after it happened, after he killed her, Mrs. L. spread that story about taking Kat to meet friends in Redding to keep people from wondering about her disappearance. She had Kat's roommates ship her things out here to stop any investigation from New York. And then, when she saw your photo in the newspaper, she thought it was a way to prove to everyone that Kat was still alive and well."

Mrs. L. lifted tormented eyes. "I never thought far enough ahead, never thought about it coming to killing you. I called Evan the day after you got here. I made that special trip into Yreka to do it because I was afraid you might overhear if I called him from here. He was angry at first. He thought identifying you as Kat and bringing you to the ranch was a stupid thing to do. But I'd already done it, so he said we'd go along with it for a while. I kept hoping you'd never remember that you were someone else, that you'd just *become* Kat. Because you were so sweet and nice and I liked you. Sometimes I even thought that maybe somehow you really *were* Kat, that Evan thought he'd killed you but somehow he'd made a mistake. And you were still alive, and somehow you'd made your way to Oregon and become nicer when you got amnesia. I know that doesn't make much sense, but…" Mrs. L.'s voice trailed off, and she wiped a trickle of tears from the corner of her eye.

No, it didn't make logical sense, Sara agreed, but she didn't doubt how desperately Mrs. L. had wanted to believe it.

"But you knew the body was buried out in the woods." Jace's voice wasn't unkind, but it was uncompromising.

Mrs. L. shook her head. "No, I didn't know. I never saw the body. I thought he'd taken it far off somewhere. But Katy found the necklace out in the woods, and then I knew the body was buried out there, and somehow everything seemed so much more terrible after I knew that."

A pang of sadness and sympathy for the real Kat swept over Sara. She hadn't been an admirable woman. She'd lived a shallow, self-centered, and misguided life. But to have it end in violence and a lonely grave in the woods…

"And then," Mrs. L. lifted her eyes to Sara's, her voice a haunted whisper, "you started to see those 'shadows.'"

How well Sara remembered the first time she had seen those shadows in her mind. Almost wistfully, because she was already almost certain of the answer, she asked, "Was there ever a Fourth of July when the Cavanaughs and Kat and Evan went to a fireworks celebration?"

Mrs. L. shook her head. "No, I just made that up. But after that night we knew you were starting to remember, and Evan wanted me to arrange an accident for you. But I just couldn't do it, so he said we'd have to do it this way. I didn't want to. I felt sick and miserable about it, and I tried and tried to think of some way not to do it. But there wasn't any way around it, and we couldn't wait until you remembered and ruined everything.

So Evan came last night, in the middle of the night, in a car he rented under a phony name. He hid it in the woods a few miles down the road. And then this morning I got you to come back to the river with me."

The car she had seen last night when she peered out the window, Sara realized. Evan, with murder on his mind.

Mrs. L. held out her hands and helplessly repeated the same words she'd spoken at the river. "I'm so sorry, Ka—" She broke off in the middle of the name, acknowledging now that it was wrong.

"I'm Sara Garrison. Almost drowning in the river brought everything about my real identity back to me."

Mrs. L. asked no questions about that other identity. She didn't even look curious, just beaten and hopeless. "Evan always did have trouble with his temper," she said, more as if she were talking to herself than them. "That was why Thornton and Mavis thought it would be best if I didn't work for them for a while when he was a teenager, and he resented that. And it hasn't been easy for him, working for that stingy company in Texas, and them so mean and unpleasant when some of the franchises he'd set up didn't work out."

Still making excuses for him, Sara realized regretfully. Just as she'd probably done all his life.

"I have to call the authorities." Jace glanced at Mrs. L., his face troubled.

She looked up, coming out of her reverie about Evan, and smiled wanly. "I'm not going anywhere. I'll just wait in my room."

Joe hesitated and then said, "I'll wait with you."

Sara curled up on the sofa in the living room, the velvet robe tucked around her bare feet, while Jace made the call. She was comfortably warm now, but a body memory of the chill of the river still lingered. After the phone call Jace reported that the authorities were on their way with a search party to look for Evan's body and someone to pick up Mrs. L.

"What will happen to her?"

"Maybe a plea bargain of some kind, because I don't think she'll deny being an accomplice to attempted murder." He came to the sofa and wrapped his arms around her. "Ka—Sara, can you forgive me for ever doubting what you said about Evan trying to kill you?"

"It must have sounded like just one more bit of craziness from someone who was already swinging on a mental teeter-totter. Can you forgive *me* for being suspicious of *you*?"

"Yes," he said instantly, even before he knew what those suspicions were.

She explained then, how she kept feeling she wasn't Kat Cavanaugh but if she wasn't, where was the real Kat? And jumping from there to a suspicion that Kat was dead and either Barry or Jace must have killed her. "I suspected Barry because she'd dumped him personally and professionally, and I knew he'd threatened to kill her. But I also suspected you, thinking you were already angry about the land deal on the ranch, and that maybe you hadn't told me the truth about you and Kat, that perhaps she had rejected you instead of the other way around, and when it happened you snapped."

"A suspicion understandably reinforced by how I lost it that day in Redding," he said ruefully.

"And I owe Joe an apology, too. I even thought he deliberately tried to run over and kill me with the van, to get rid of me and protect you."

Jace shook his head. "And you had all this closed up inside you, carrying it all alone."

"Until I let myself lean on the Lord."

"I'm glad about that, so very glad. I always knew you would eventually. I could feel it every time you tried to claim disbelief and lack of faith."

"But this changes everything, doesn't it?"

"Such as?"

"Us."

"It doesn't change that I love you!"

"You can't know you love me! You don't know anything about me as Sara Garrison."

"I didn't fall in love with Kat or Katy Cavanaugh. I fell in love with the woman behind the name, the woman I almost lost today. *You*."

"I'm not a New York model. I don't own the ranch. I—"

"Does it matter to *you* that you're not a New York model? That you don't own the ranch?" he challenged.

"No!"

"Then why should it matter to me?"

She floundered, uncertain why it should matter but certain it must.

"Do you love me?" he demanded.

"Oh, yes!"

"Then the rest of it is all just minor details to fill in the blanks. Some of which you might fill in for me right now." He changed positions, pulling her into his arms so her back rested against his bare chest, as if he were settling down to give them all the time they needed.

"I hardly know where to start."

"How about at the beginning, with, 'I was born in…'?" He ended on an upnote and nuzzled her cheek, encouraging her to fill in the blank.

"I was born in Texas," she began slowly. "To wonderful Christian parents. My father was in the military, and my mother always loved doing anything with plants, working in a flower shop or greenhouse or tree nursery. We moved around a lot, of course, with Dad in the military, so I never had any real hometown or longtime friends, but maybe that just brought us closer as a family. Then, when I was in high school and Dad was stationed in Korea, they adopted a little Korean girl who'd lost her parents. Her name was Kimsi, but we always called her Cricket because when she got excited she made this sweet, funny little chirpy noise." Sara smiled reminiscently, her throat closing up with bittersweet memory of the adopted sister she had loved so dearly.

"Cricket!" Jace exclaimed, understanding dawning.

"She had some emotional problems at first, but we all loved her so much and by the time we came back to the States and she'd learned to trust us, she'd become the sweetest, most wonderful little girl. Then I started college."

"And studied computers?" Jace guessed.

She shook her head. "No, I planned to be a teacher, although I also took some computer classes. But in my sophomore year, my parents were killed in a boat accident on the Mississippi River."

"Oh, Ka—Sara, I'm so sorry!"

"Maybe that was why Katy's loss of her parents seemed so much like a real part of me," Sara said softly. "Even now I almost feel as if they were a beloved aunt and uncle I've lost."

Jace just held her close, his jaw pressed hard against her cheek in silent comfort.

"Cricket was only seven when it happened. It was a terrible blow for both of us, but we shared a wonderful faith in the Lord and had him to lean on. Then another blow hit when the authorities tried to take Cricket away and put her in a foster home. My parents had named me to take care of her if anything happened to them, but the authorities fought it because I wasn't twenty-one yet, too young in their eyes. As if strangers could care for her better than I could! But I vowed they weren't going to separate us. I found a woman lawyer to fight them, which she did by getting herself named guardian for both of us. Then, when I turned twenty-one, she arranged legal custody of Cricket for me."

"She sounds like a wonderful woman," Jace said thoughtfully. "But why wasn't she looking for you while you thought you were Kat?"

"Because a month after she finished our case, she was killed in a carjacking out in her office parking lot." Sara hesitated, remembering the shock of that, and finally added slowly, "Which, even though my faith didn't fail then, was maybe when I first began to question God's love and caring."

"What about college?"

"I kept going. It wasn't easy managing time and money so I could take care of Cricket and attend classes, too. In fact, we lived a kind of leap-from-one-crisis-to-the-next kind of life. But it was a wonderful time anyway. We had each other and the Lord." Sara brushed away tears, remembering the sweet closeness they'd shared. "And then Cricket got sick."

Jace didn't say anything, but she could feel his sudden dismay, as if he realized something even worse was coming.

"It didn't seem too serious at first. Headaches and tiredness. The doctor thought it was the tail end of a flu that wouldn't go away. Then, like some monster creeping up from inside her, she started having trouble with her eyesight, then her hearing and speech. Finally, through an MRI and biopsy, they diagnosed it as..." Sara closed her eyes as her mind dragged up the letters one by one until they spelled the strange and terrifying word. "Rhabdomyosarcoma. It's a type of cancer, and the tumor was so close to vital nerves in her head that they couldn't do surgery, and the other treatments, radiation and chemotherapy, were horrendous. I quit college then, of course, to take care of her, and we moved to Minnesota to be near a clinic and specialist."

"But they couldn't help her?" Jace asked softly.

"They tried. Tried very hard. But she suffered so much, from treatments as well as disease. Oh, Jace, how she suffered! I couldn't stand it. I kept praying to God to keep her from suffering so much, to help her somehow, but he didn't seem to be listening. By then the money was running out, so I took in computer work I could do at home and still take care of her. Then, like some miracle, she got a little better! Tests showed the tumor had shrunk. I cheered. I praised God! I thought she was on her way to healing! And then they discovered she wasn't better at all, that she had bone cancer and needed a bone-marrow transplant. And I wasn't a match, of course, so I couldn't donate to her. Then there was more pain, and all I could do was watch her suffer, and wonder why God didn't care."

"Oh, honey." She could feel his pain as he absorbed hers.

"She died while we were still trying to find a matching donor. All her pain, all that suffering, all in vain." Sara shook her head helplessly. "And I just collapsed and went wild at the same time. I hated God, not just for taking her, but for making her suffer so much first. I couldn't understand how he could heap so much on one innocent little girl. Taking her real parents and then her adopted parents too, then snatching even this woman who had helped us. As if he were out to get anyone important to either of us! Stealing Cricket's eyesight and hearing, putting her through so *much* suffering for one so young and helpless. I can still hear her crying in the night."

Jace rocked her gently as she buried her face in her hands and let the tears fall. The tears didn't end then, but she spoke through them in broken words.

"And after she was gone, all I wanted was to get away, away

from everything. So I sold my computer and everything else I couldn't stuff in the car and just started driving. I didn't know where I was going and didn't care. Mostly I just wanted to out-run God, I think. Abandon and reject him the way he'd abandoned and rejected Cricket when she needed him most.

"I got to Seattle, and the car broke down. I remember thinking bitterly, 'Thanks, God, you're all heart, aren't you?' All my life I'd believed in a loving, caring God, and now I believed that, if he existed at all, he was cruel and uncaring. The repair bill was more than the car was worth, so I just walked off and left it and everything in it. Then I happened to overhear some people in a store talking about taking a camping trip by bicycle down the Oregon coast that summer. I thought, why not? I guess it's a good thing I didn't overhear people talking about a slow freighter to the Orient, or I might have wound up in some strange foreign place rather than here," she added with an effort to lighten her grim story.

"No, God intended you for here, for me." Jace's voice held no trace of doubt. "And he did indeed work in mysterious ways to get you here, didn't he?"

"I took a bus down to Portland, bought some camping equipment and a bicycle, rode over to the coast, and started down Highway 101. It's a popular trip with bicyclists, and there are campgrounds all along the coast. This was earlier in the year than most people do it by bicycle, but the weather was good, and I met a few other bicyclists along the way. The coast scenery was wild and spectacular, but I just resented God for that, too. Then, somewhere along the southern coast, I took an old side road up into the hills thinking I'd camp up there somewhere that night."

"All by yourself, not in a campground?"

She smiled wryly. "I was tired of friendly, helpful people concerned about a woman traveling alone. Anyway, it was a steep climb, and I rounded a curve and saw a bridge. Then the sun hit my eyes and blinded me, and the bike swerved into gravel beside the bridge. I remember both me and the bike flying through the air and landing in brush, and then I was tumbling, falling, hitting something. Then it was like today, being tossed and whirled, as if the whole world had become a maelstrom of water. After that my memory is still gone, but I think I must have washed down the creek to the beach, then sloshed in the surf until someone found me."

Jace nodded slowly. "Your bicycle and identification are probably still hidden in brush somewhere alongside an old road in Oregon."

"And I woke up in the Benton Beach Hospital and became Kat Cavanaugh."

"And I fell in love with you." He reached up and erased the trail of teardrops across her cheek with a fingertip. "Is it too soon to talk about marriage, Ka—Sara?"

"Maybe it's too soon until you learn to call me by my real name," she teased through the tears.

"I love you, Sara Garrison," he said fiercely. "I love you, and I want to marry you."

"But there's still something I have to do." The thing she hadn't been able to bring herself to do before her memory fled into the darkness.

Twenty - Three

They stood at the foot of the grave, the September sunlight golden in this rural midwestern cemetery. Around them the other gravestones were mostly older, weathered, yet lovingly cared for. The chrysanthemums they had placed on the two adjoining graves glowed orange and rust and gold against the dark green of grass.

It was accomplished now, this thing she had fled from doing yet couldn't escape, this thing that had haunted her even in the dark emptiness of lost memory. Sadness and gladness that Cricket was beyond suffering now, safe in the arms of the Lord, mingled in her mind and heart.

Jace's arm held her shoulders with fierce tenderness as they studied the words engraved on the newly erected rose-granite stone.

KIMSI GARRISON
Our Beloved Cricket

"Do you wonder why I didn't do it before?" Sara asked. "Why I left the grave without a headstone when she was first buried here?"

Jace silently pressed his cheek against her temple.

"It was because it was such a final gesture, a good-bye I couldn't make. It was as if, once the stone with her name was erected, it would be an admission that she was gone forever. And so I rejected the God who had taken her and ran away instead of accepting the eternal truth that those we love are never truly gone forever, that for believers there will someday be a happy reunion. Now I'm just grateful I had her as long as I did."

Sara knelt and placed the third bouquet of chrysanthemums in the container in front of the gravestone. "Good-bye, Cricket," she said softly. "We'll meet again."

At the gate in the stone fence surrounding the old cemetery, she paused and looked back. Sara had never known the grandparents who were buried here, nor had Cricket, but there was a family unity in the three graves placed side by side, a peaceful serenity there beneath the trees with leaves just beginning to show a blaze of fall color. Sara's own parents were buried in a military cemetery, and so this was where she had chosen for Cricket. Now it was finished, and she felt the peace of completion that had so long been missing.

They flew back to Redding and picked up Jace's pickup at the airport, talking little but taking comfort in each other's nearness. The crisp air of coming fall made the lingering warmth of summer doubly sweet as they drove through the mountains, but Sara felt a returning twinge of sadness when they passed the driveway to the log house she had once thought of as home. The strips of yellow plastic across the driveway that marked the ranch as a crime scene were gone now, and the house looked lonely, brooding, and abandoned, Mrs. L.'s garden and rose bushes dry and forlorn.

So sad, Sara thought with a pang, all that had happened there. So strange how love could have gone so wrong in the tangled relationships between man and woman, mother and son.

But just across the road, at Damascus, a different mood prevailed. Noisy shouts echoed from a football game in progress, and a chain saw buzzed beyond the woodpile. Joe's welcoming wave came from under the van, where he was busy with the unending process of keeping the old vehicle running. The cats, Maggie and Tillie, who had made the move to the school with relative tranquillity, lazed like furry doorstops beside the dormitory door. And a corporate donation of twenty cases of bean sprouts crowded the kitchen steps.

Jace laughed. "I hope you like Chinese food. I have a feeling we may be eating a lot of it."

He lifted her suitcase from the back of the pickup, and she led the way upstairs to her room in the staff wing of the dormitory where she had lived since leaving the ranch. At the doorway she turned, and Jace draped his arms around her.

"Welcome home," he said. He smiled and kissed her lightly.

Home, Sara thought with a feeling of wonder followed by a sweet rush of satisfaction and relief and happiness. Yes, *home*. "Thank you for going with me," she whispered.

"That's what a husband-to-be is for, to be there when the woman he loves needs him." He smiled. "A husband-to-be who is eager to change that to just plain *husband* whenever you're ready."

One part of Sara recklessly said *Yes! Let's do it now, right now, before another day goes by!* Jace had suggested they be married before they flew to the midwest to put the headstone on Cricket's grave. But now, as then, another part of Sara held back. Not for lack of love. Oh, no! She didn't doubt the depths of her love for him, or his for her. She felt that love whether she was in his arms or miles away, whether, as now, their eyes were only inches apart or their gazes met across a dining room crowded with boys, whether they were worshipping together in the chapel or slinging overripe zucchini and laughter at each other in the garden.

It was just that she still needed time to put her interrupted life back together, to mend the strange rip in the continuity of her existence, to look to the future instead of the past. "Soon," she whispered.

"I'm ready whenever you are. Just remember, I love you, Sara."

She tilted her head back to look into his loving eyes. "At least you get my name right these days," she teased lightly. "You don't slip and call me Katy anymore."

"I love you whether you're Katy or Sara or Judy Jones from Juneau. All I want to do with your name is make it end in *Foster.*"

Sara thought about those words as she stood at her window that night and looked across the road at the dark silhouette of the log house. Its ownership was in limbo at the moment, but Jace planned to make an offer on it whenever the legal details were straightened out. Sara had accepted Jace's invitation to live and work at Damascus as soon as she realized she wasn't Kat Cavanaugh and didn't belong there at the ranch. Kat's shallow grave in the woods had been found a few days after Evan's body was pulled from the river, and Mrs. L.'s future, now that she had suffered a nervous breakdown, was up in the air. Joe faithfully went to visit her once a week.

Sara threw herself into activities of the school and her job, straightening and organizing records and files that Jace admitted, with gross understatement, were a bit disorganized. She checked with the university she'd attended and found what it would take to get her degree and become a teacher here at the school. She wrote Barry and explained everything that had happened, but she never heard from him and could only wonder if he mourned the real Kat or simply dismissed her as being of no more use to him.

Slowly the part of her that had almost become Kat receded, and she was fully Sara once more.

And one day in early November, as she and Jace picked the last of the late apples in the school's little orchard, he wrapped his arms around her from behind so they could share crisp bites from the same apple. "Ready for a wedding?" he asked softly.

Sara tilted her head at him and smiled. Yes, she was ready.

And so it was, on the day after Thanksgiving, that Sara Garrison, in long white gown, walked down the aisle of the chapel on the arm of a delighted Dr. Fischer. Standing at the altar waiting for her was Jace, expression solemn in the flickering candlelight but eyes joyously alight with love. They joined hands as Mac repeated the timeless words that made them one before God.

Then they were walking back down the aisle together as husband and wife, passing through a double line of Damascus boys in various stages of solemnity and giggles, Ramsey mischievously giving them a surreptitious thumbs-up sign. Walking into their future knowing they had been led to each other by the Lord, who never forgot.

Dear Reader:

One of the questions writers are most frequently asked is, "Where do you get your ideas?" Usually I can't supply a solid answer to that question; the origin of an idea seems to be lost in a misty haze. Perhaps something in the news will jiggle the creative spot in my brain, or sometimes it's a conversation or some incident from my own experience. An intriguing question may pop into a writer's head, or a connection may be made between unrelated incidents or people. But mostly, I think, ideas for my Christian fiction have come because the Lord has opened my eyes to something or made me see a situation from a different viewpoint. A pastor's message may offer fresh insight or a familiar Bible verse may suddenly jump out at me with new meaning.

Forgotten is one of the few books for which I can actually pinpoint where the idea came from. Some years back I read in the newspaper about a man who was in a hospital with amnesia. Because of media publicity about his situation, a relative identified him and took him home. Happy ending. However, a question nagged at me. Could anyone have identified and claimed him as a relative? What if the relative made a mistake—or had an ulterior motive for making the identification? Yet, at the moment, that was as far as the "idea" went. It simply languished somewhere in the back of my mind. It wasn't until some years later, after the Lord had led me to writing Christian fiction, that, seemingly out of nowhere, I saw a connection between forgetting the past and feeling forgotten by God. And from that came this story.

I hope you enjoy it, and know that you, too, are never forgotten by the Lord.

Lorena McCourtney

You may write to Lorena McCourtney
c/o Multnomah Publishers
P.O. Box 1720
Sisters, Oregon 97759

PALISADES...PURE ROMANCE

~ PALISADES ~

Reunion, Karen Ball
Refuge, Lisa Tawn Bergren
Torchlight, Lisa Tawn Bergren
Treasure, Lisa Tawn Bergren
Chosen, Lisa Tawn Bergren
Firestorm, Lisa Tawn Bergren
Surrender, Lynn Bulock
Wise Man's House, Melody Carlson
Heartland Skies, Melody Carlson (March 1998)
Cherish, Constance Colson
Chase the Dream, Constance Colson
Angel Valley, Peggy Darty
Sundance, Peggy Darty
Moonglow, Peggy Darty
Promises, Peggy Darty
Memories, Peggy Darty (May 1998)
Remembering the Roses, Marion Duckworth (June 1998)
Love Song, Sharon Gillenwater
Antiques, Sharon Gillenwater
Texas Tender, Sharon Gillenwater
Secrets, Robin Jones Gunn
Whispers, Robin Jones Gunn
Echoes, Robin Jones Gunn
Sunsets, Robin Jones Gunn
Clouds, Robin Jones Gunn
Waterfalls, Robin Jones Gunn
Coming Home, Barbara Jean Hicks
Snow Swan, Barbara Jean Hicks
China Doll, Barbara Jean Hicks (June 1998)
Angel in the Senate, Kristen Johnson Ingram (March 1998)
Irish Eyes, Annie Jones
Father by Faith, Annie Jones

Irish Rogue, Annie Jones
Glory, Marilyn Kok
Sierra, Shari MacDonald
Forget-Me-Not, Shari MacDonald
Diamonds, Shari MacDonald
Stardust, Shari MacDonald
Westward, Amanda MacLean
Stonehaven, Amanda MacLean
Everlasting, Amanda MacLean
Kingdom Come, Amanda MacLean
Betrayed, Lorena McCourtney
Escape, Lorena McCourtney
Dear Silver, Lorena McCourtney
Forgotten, Lorena McCourtney
Enough! Gayle Roper
The Key, Gayle Roper (April 1998)
Voyage, Elaine Schulte

⁓ ANTHOLOGIES ⁓

A Christmas Joy, Darty, Gillenwater, MacLean
Mistletoe, Ball, Hicks, McCourtney
A Mother's Love, Bergren, Colson, MacLean
Silver Bells, Bergren, Krause, MacDonald
Heart's Delight, Ball, Hicks, Noble
Fools for Love, Ball, Brooks, Jones (March 1998)